NEW ZEALAND'S GREAT WHITE SHARKS

DEDICATED TO MICHAEL MANNING (1973–2009)

Michael Manning loved sharks. He loved learning about them, working with them, and telling stories about them to his young daughter, Caitlin, and her friends at preschool.

Michael was a marine biologist who was also good with numbers, and he combined these interests to work out the populations of different fish species. He worked at the National Institute of Water and Atmospheric Research (NIWA) from 2001–2009 and, along with Malcolm Francis and Clinton Duffy, helped kick off the New Zealand great white shark project in 2005. The team worked at the Chatham Islands and Stewart Island, using electronic tags to find out where sharks go. Michael tagged four sharks, including Caitlin, who he named after his daughter.

In 2009, Michael and his family moved to New Caledonia. He was keen to try and tag great white sharks there as well but, sadly, that never happened. Michael died from a heart defect that he didn't know he had. This book is dedicated to Michael's memory, and the Michael Manning Memorial Trust has gifted copies of it to schools in New Zealand and the South Pacific.

NEW ZEALAND'S GREAT WHITE SHARKS

How science is revealing their secrets

ALISON BALLANCE

pb potton & burton

CONTENTS

1 THE GREAT WHITE SHARK PUZZLE — 8
Nicholas Cage Sets Off — 9
Keeping an Eye on Sharks — 10
The Great White Shark Project Team — 11
The Great White Shark Project Begins — 14
Tools of the Trade — 16

2 PLAYING TAG — 18
Nature of the Beast — 24
Who Are You? — 26

3 PATTING SHARKS: ELLA GOES NORTH AND SOUTH — 28
Lost and Found — 31
How Old is that Shark? — 32

4 LISTENING FOR SHARKS — 34
Nicholas Cage Earns His Name — 36
The Stewart Island Shark Gang — 38
On the Menu — 40

5 SHARK SPOTTING — 42
Built for the Kill — 46

6 AN OCEAN JOURNEY — 48
How Sharks Navigate — 50
Diving Deep — 55
Where in the World — 56

7 HEADING HOME — 58
Great White Shark Attacks — 61

8 THE AUSTRALIAN CONNECTION — 62
Tracking Pip — 62
The Australian Great White Shark Project — 64
Australia's Shark Nurseries — 65
New Zealand's Young Sharks — 66
How DNA Can Help Us Understand White Sharks — 67

9 MOTHERS AND BABIES — 68
Shark Sex — 68
Pregnant Great Whites — 69
Baby Sharks — 70

10 PIP RETURNS — 72
The Numbers Game — 77

11 PIECES OF THE PUZZLE — 78
What We Know — 78
Unsolved Puzzle Pieces — 79

ACKNOWLEDGEMENTS — 80

GLOSSARY — 81

INDEX — 82

PHOTO CREDITS — 84

Chapter 1
THE GREAT WHITE SHARK PUZZLE

Everybody knows what a great white shark is, but what do we know about their lives and how they behave?

We know surprisingly little about them because great white sharks are hard to study.

Why? Because there's not many of them, they move around a lot in the ocean, and they don't have to come to the surface to breathe. This means we get just occasional glimpses of only a few of them, and it's difficult to learn much from these brief encounters.

Studying great white sharks is like doing a big jigsaw puzzle, where you've got only a few pieces and you don't know what the picture looks like.

In this book we're going on a journey with some scientists to find out how much we know about New Zealand's great white sharks, and we'll uncover lots of shark secrets along the way.

We'll fill in some pieces of the shark puzzle and discover what pieces are still missing. And we'll be finding out how science works.

It'll be exciting, so let's go.

NICHOLAS CAGE SETS OFF

From: Malcolm Francis, NIWA
To: Clinton Duffy, Kina Scollay
Sent: 2 July 2013
Subject: Nicholas Cage

Nicholas Cage is romping away! Currently pointed at about Norfolk Island.

Shark scientist Malcolm Francis is in his office in Wellington.

Fellow shark scientist Clinton Duffy is in Auckland.

Film-maker and shark expert Kina Scollay is in Picton.

And Nicholas Cage, a 3.5-metre male great white shark, is swimming north. He left Stewart Island five days earlier, and the scientists have no idea where he is going. But he is being closely monitored. Each time he swims near the surface and his tall dorsal fin rises out of the water, a small piece of spyware attached to the tip of the fin – a SPOT tag – tells passing satellites where he is.

He's still in New Zealand waters but at some point in the next few days, Nicholas Cage (Nic for short) will cross into international waters. He might be heading across the Tasman Sea to Australia, or he could head north into the Pacific Ocean, to Norfolk Island perhaps, or even further north to New Caledonia.

One thing is certain: he will remain under constant surveillance by these shark experts who are keenly interested to know his destination.

Nicholas Cage, a 3.5-metre male great white shark.

KEEPING AN EYE ON SHARKS

We used to think that great white sharks were found only in cool coastal waters and that they were stay-at-home fish. But we were wrong. Placing electronic tags on sharks has opened our eyes to their world by telling us what they do and where they go when we aren't looking.

In 1999, shark scientists in Australia and the United States started using electronic tags on great whites for the first time.

Tagging soon revealed that great white sharks don't just stay near the coast. Four tagged white sharks from California swam out into the middle of the Pacific Ocean. One even went to Hawaii; before this there had been only a few rare records of white sharks from there. It was an amazing revelation.

Shark scientists around the world were inspired to use the same technology to learn about their own sharks, and in 2005 a Kiwi team began the New Zealand great white shark project.

THE GREAT WHITE SHARK PROJECT TEAM

CLINTON DUFFY

Clinton Duffy knows exactly when he first got hooked on sharks: he was four years old and was on holiday with his family. He saw a shark fin slicing through the water near the boat he was a passenger in.

From that moment he became obsessed with sharks and wouldn't stop talking and thinking about them. He remembers adults telling him that there were no sharks in New Zealand as the waters were too cold – but he'd seen one, and he knew that wasn't true.

The first time the team went to the Chatham Islands, Clinton got into a shark cage to be in the water with great whites. He's never wanted to do it again. He says that the sharks had an eerie ability to appear out of nowhere and just be there, peering through the bars of the shark cage at him.

What sticks in his mind about seeing white sharks underwater is their bulk. 'They are just so much bigger than you imagine. We talk about how long they are, but that doesn't tell you anything about their sheer bulk and mass.'

Clinton collects sightings of great white sharks in New Zealand. He keeps newspaper clippings, fishing club reports, anything he can find. After 25 years he has a large and very useful set of great white shark records.

Clinton works for the Department of Conservation, researching sharks and other marine issues.

Clinton Duffy about to return a school shark to the water.

MALCOLM FRANCIS

Malcolm Francis has always been mad about fish. And the best kind of fish? Sharks, of course. As a young teenager he borrowed every library book that featured sharks. As well as reading about them, Malcolm copied out entire chapters, by hand, into an exercise book. This was before the internet and photocopiers, and these hand-written notes were his shark bible.

Malcolm learnt to snorkel when he was 13 years old and to scuba dive when he was 17 years old. It took four years to fulfil his wish to see a live shark in the wild, because he says you just don't see sharks very often when diving around New Zealand.

Malcolm describes great white sharks as curious, cautious, and graceful. After working with them for 11 years he has seen more than a hundred white sharks, but he never gets tired of them.

He's always thrilled when a new email pops up in his inbox to update him of the whereabouts of a tagged shark. He often wonders what they're doing, and worries when he doesn't hear from them.

Malcolm is a fisheries biologist at the National Institute of Water and Atmospheric Research (NIWA). He is a keen diver who likes taking photographs of fish.

KINA SCOLLAY

Kina Scollay was diving for paua at the Chatham Islands in 1996 when he was attacked by a great white shark. His fellow divers kept him alive until he could be flown to hospital in New Zealand and he made a full recovery.

He says that after the attack he needed to learn more about great white sharks to try and understand what had happened. He was surprised to find that no one in New Zealand knew anything about them, and he became very interested in finding out more.

He began talking with shark scientists and film-makers, and he says, 'If I had been able to find the answers easily, I wouldn't have been so fascinated.'

A couple of years after the attack he helped make a TV documentary about great whites at the Chatham Islands. He designed a shark cage and then, even though he was very nervous, he dived in it so he could see a great white shark underwater.

'It was mind-blowing,' Kina says. 'The sheer size and bulk of a great white is staggering.'

Kina still dives, and is more fascinated with white sharks than ever. As well as filming for the New Zealand great white shark project, he makes shark and underwater documentaries.

THE GREAT WHITE SHARK PROJECT BEGINS

In 2005, Malcolm and Clinton first went to the Chatham Islands. They had been told there were plenty of great whites there, especially in autumn.

Kina introduced the team to local Chatham Island fisher, Tim Gregory-Hunt, who used to take people out to fish for sharks. But he began to realise he didn't want to kill them anymore; he wanted to find out about them.

Mexican shark scientist Ramon Bonfil came along to help. Ramon had been tagging sharks in South Africa. He was part of the team who tagged the famous shark Nicole, a sub-adult female who swam from South Africa to Western Australia in early 2004.

Tim took the team in his boat to some small, remote islands called the Star Keys/Motuhope. There is a breeding colony of New Zealand fur seals there, and it is where Kina was attacked. Over two days in April 2005, the team successfully tagged their first sharks with electronic PAT tags.

Malcolm and Clinton were stunned when they found out where the sharks had travelled: a 4.2-metre female called Tessa swam to the Louisville Ridge near the Kermadec Islands; a 3.2-metre male called Tristan went to Vanuatu; and Meca, a 4-metre female travelled to New Caledonia.

For the first time, the team found out that New Zealand white sharks are international travellers that make long journeys and spend lots of time in warm tropical water. They were excited, but they had many more questions. How long did sharks stay in the tropics? Did they come back to the Chatham Islands? And did they return to the same place in the Pacific each year? To answer these questions they needed to tag more sharks.

In 2006, the team went back to the Chatham Islands, but they didn't tag a single shark. So in 2007 they tried Stewart Island instead, and that was very successful. They went back to the Chatham Islands in 2008 and tagged six more sharks, but they decided it was much easier to work at Stewart Island. The sharks there are closer to the shore and shelter, and there are more days of better weather to go out in the boat.

Michael Manning throws a bait to lure sharks close to the boat so Clinton Duffy can take photos.

In the first year of tagging at the Chatham Islands, the team used a body board as one of the ways to attract sharks. This was something that South African researchers also used for a while, as well as floating foam cut out in the shape of a seal.

The first great white sharks tagged in New Zealand at the Chatham Islands surprised everyone – instead of being stay-at-homes who liked cool water, their electronic tags revealed them to be international travellers who enjoyed hanging out in the tropical Pacific.

Tessa = blue
Tristan = orange
Meca = green

TOOLS OF THE TRADE

The New Zealand great white shark project used three kinds of electronic tags.

PAT tags and acoustic tags are designed to be streamlined and sit in the flow of water along the shark's body.

PAT tag (Pop-up Archival Transmitting tag)
Cost: $5500

A PAT tag tells you where a shark has gone and how deep it dived. It stores information on date, time, depth, water temperature and light levels.

A PAT tag is easy to use. It's like giving the shark an injection – the tag is quickly darted into thick muscle on the shark's back, near the big dorsal fin.

At a pre-programmed time a pin corrodes, allowing the tag to detach from the shark and 'pop up' to the sea surface. As it bobs around it 'talks' with passing satellites and sends data. Until the tag pops up you have no idea where the shark has been.

Scientists use the recorded light levels to estimate the times of dawn, midday and dusk. From this, they can work out the shark's approximate route, accurate to within about 100 kilometres.

Thirty-six sharks were tagged with PAT tags at Stewart Island and the Chatham Islands between 2005 and 2014. Some were tagged more than once.

SPOT tag (Smart Position or Temperature Transmitting tag)

Cost: $2400

A SPOT tag gives an accurate position of a shark, in real time. It transmits a location to a satellite every time the shark comes to the surface. It doesn't store any data.

Because the scientists must catch the shark and attach the tag to its dorsal fin, a SPOT tag is not easy to use. The bolts that hold the tag in place are meant to eventually corrode so the tag falls off and the holes in the shark's fin heal over.

Five sharks were tagged with SPOT tags at Stewart Island: Livie (whose tag failed after a few days), Grim, Nicholas Cage, Pip and Caro.

Acoustic tag

Cost: $400

Acoustic tags are useful for finding out where sharks go in a small area, such as around Stewart Island. Each tag has a unique 'ping', and when a shark gets closer than about 500 metres that ping is detected by special listening stations positioned in the water. The listening station records the date, time and identification of every shark nearby.

Acoustic tags are attached the same way as PAT tags.

Forty-five Stewart Island sharks were tagged with acoustic tags in 2011 and 2012.

Warrick Lyon holds an acoustic listening station ready to be put in the water near Stewart Island.

Chapter 2
PLAYING TAG

It's 8 o'clock on a calm morning, in autumn 2011.

Scientists Malcolm, Clinton and Kina arrive at Halfmoon Bay wharf, at Stewart Island, where the Department of Conservation boat Hananui *is already waiting. The team have tagged 21 sharks in the last fortnight, and they have just two days left to use the remaining six tags. They load their equipment onto the boat and, a few minutes later, they are casting off the ropes. Meadsy, the skipper, is at the helm. With a deep throaty rumble, the boat makes its way slowly past the ferry and fishing boats moored in the bay.*

They are heading to the east side of Edwards Island, in the Titi Islands group. The boat picks up speed as it leaves the harbour and the three men are already unpacking their equipment and getting ready for what they hope will be a long and busy day.

Clinton's first job is to make up the berley, an oily, stinky brew that will attract sharks from several kilometres away. He then wraps one end of a long rope tightly around a dead tuna, and knots it securely. It will be used as bait, to lure sharks close enough to the boat in order for them to be tagged. Clinton knows that without the added incentive of a tasty tuna, many sharks wouldn't be bold enough to swim up alongside the boat.

Malcolm is setting up the tagging pole that will be used to dart tags into the sharks' backs.

Kina puts his video camera into a watertight underwater housing unit and attaches it to the end of a long metal pole.

The half-hour trip passes quickly and Meadsy is soon dropping anchor at their favourite sharky place. The most sharks Clinton and Malcolm have ever seen here in one day is 15, but there have also been days when they haven't seen any.

The water here is about 18 metres deep, and they are about 250 metres offshore from Edwards Island and its colony of breeding New Zealand fur seals. The seals are why the sharks hang out here – a seal pup that hasn't properly learnt to keep an eye out for danger makes a great meal for a hungry predator.

It's time to call in the sharks. Malcolm ladles berley over the side of the boat. A few litres of berley might not seem a lot in a whole ocean, but great white sharks are very sensitive to smell. This odour trail could be attracting the attention of sharks that are several kilometres away.

Seabirds also have a keen sense of smell. Within five minutes, 10 small albatrosses have settled on the water, watching for any pieces of fish to go with the tantalising aroma. Several barracouta also mill around.

Everyone keeps an eye out, knowing that sharks will appear out of the tidal rip to the north, where the berley trail is slowly drifting.

An hour passes. Nothing. Two hours, then three. The team has lunch. They run out of berley and make up some more.

Suddenly one, then another, albatross lifts off the water. By the time four of these early warning shark detectors have taken to the air, the team knows that there's definitely a shark on its way. Then, a hundred metres from the boat, a dark fin breaks the surface of the water. It's the tip of a great white shark's tail. It slices

Stewart Island great white shark berley recipe: Into a fish bin add raw minced-up tuna, blood (if you have any) and a generous dollop of concentrated tuna oil (the label on the bottle describes it as 'The Ultimate Enticer'). Dilute with seawater. Mix well. Ladle generously into the sea.

An acoustic tag is loaded onto the end of the tagging pole, ready for action.

a slow, sinuous curve through the water then disappears as the shark slips gently beneath the water's surface.

The arrival of the shark sets off a flurry of activity on the boat.

Clinton throws the tuna bait and its rope as far as he can out into the water, then he begins to slowly pull it back towards the boat.

Kina places the pole camera into the water. He wears a helmet with an eye piece that takes a video feed from his camera so he can see the underwater action. He rotates the pole and the camera, looking for the shark.

Malcolm has a PAT tag loaded onto the end of his tagging pole. He waits on the main deck of the boat, ready to step onto the duckboard with Kina and Clinton if a shark comes close enough.

All eyes are on the water. They know that the shark will most likely approach from below, so what they're looking for is a dark shape. But sharks don't usually rush in. Many are curious but shy and will keep their distance as they size up the situation.

It's quiet. Just the gentle slap of water against the boat, the occasional distant seal call from the island, and the splash of the tuna bait being pulled in and thrown out again. Kina swivels the camera back and forth to get a good all-round view.

Suddenly Kina shouts, 'It's coming from under the boat! Watch out for the bait.'

Clinton just manages to pull the tuna bait clear before a huge head surges up in a mass of water and bubbles. Its gaping mouth snaps shut a few centimetres from where the tuna had been. Then, with an enormous flick of its tail, it twists away from the boat and dives.

Again, Kina, with his video view under the boat, alerts the crew: 'It's coming back along the port side.'

Over 4 metres of sleek muscle powers along the side of the boat. The shark is at the surface, slightly twisted onto its side. An unblinking eye looks up at the people staring back. It takes lazy aim at the tuna bait, but Clinton pulls it out of reach. The shark dives again beneath the surface and quickly disappears.

Kina swivels the video camera, following it out of sight. 'I've got footage of its right side,' he says, 'but I still need to get its left side. And I can't see any claspers so it's a female – I'm sure of that.'

Everyone on the boat is alert and watching while Clinton retrieves the bait, throws it out and pulls it back in. The minutes tick by.

'She's turning and coming back,' says Kina. 'I've got a shot of her left side now. Are you ready, Malcolm?'

Malcolm steps down to join Clinton and Kina on the duckboard, with the long tagging pole ready. As Clinton pulls the bait slowly alongside, the shark surges up from below, her back breaking the surface just a metre or so away from the men. Clinton snatches the bait from the shark's open jaws while Malcolm leans forward and stabs the tag into the thick muscle behind the shark's dorsal fin. He pulls the tagging pole back as the shark twists and thrashes.

She dives again, sending a surge of water across the duckboard.

'The tag went in just behind the fin, right where it should be,' says Malcolm. 'But now my gumboot is filled with water!'

Malcolm tags a shark.

'I recognise that shark,' says Clinton. 'That's Ella, and we've tagged her before. But she's grown – I reckon she's 4.4 metres long now.'

Malcolm and Kina nod their heads in agreement. The three of them have got very good at estimating the size of sharks around the boat, and Ella is now as long as the boat is wide.

Meadsy fills in the tagging record: '2.20pm. Ella. Female. 4.4 metres long. PAT tag number 55688.'

Everyone resumes their vigil for another large shadow in the water, albatrosses taking off or a fin breaking the surface. They ladle more berley into the water.

Suddenly, after 45 minutes, there's a loud shout of 'Shark!' as a smaller shark appears, snapping at the tuna bait and managing to bite off a small piece.

Spurred on by that success, the bold shark is soon back looking for more tuna. After a couple of passes, Kina announces he has a good video shot of each side. These photos will allow Clinton to identify the shark again in the future.

Malcolm steps down onto the duckboard, and Clinton begins to lure the shark towards the boat. The little shark is fast and agile and almost immediately appears from below. But this time he has a different target in sight – attracted by the electrical field it is emitting, the shark aims directly at the underwater video camera. Kina manages to pull the camera out of the water just before the shark's open mouth reaches it. 'That was close,' he says, laughing. 'I don't need any more tooth marks on my camera housing.'

Undeterred by its constant misses, the persistent shark tries again and again to reach the bait. Frustratingly for Malcolm, the shark's back is always just out of reach or at an awkward angle. But finally the shark is lined up at a perfect angle to the boat. 'Get ready, Malcolm,' calls Clinton. 'Here it comes.'

The shark launches its attack at the bait. Its head comes out of the water so close to the boat that the men can see its eye roll back in its socket for protection. Malcolm darts the acoustic tag into its back as it arches out of the water. The shark bucks sideways, hitting the boat and sending a wave of water across the duckboard.

'It's a male,' reports Clinton. '2.8 metres long. Just a young one. For a small shark, he's got attitude, though.'

It's taken until nearly 4.30 in the afternoon to get two tags onto two sharks. The team hope that another untagged shark might turn up, but it's clear that the young shark has not been put off by the experience of being tagged. He is hanging around, working hard to get the bait. Again and again, Clinton quickly pulls in the tuna bait to avoid it being eaten, but eventually he isn't fast enough and the shark's persistence pays off. With a quick grab and shake, he sinks his teeth into the tuna and escapes with about half of it. It's time to head back to shore.

Not every tagged shark gets a name, but the bold youngster is the one the team will come to know as Nicholas Cage, and we'll be hearing more about him later in the book.

NATURE OF THE BEAST

Carcharodon carcharias, great white shark, white shark, white pointer, makō (or mangō) taniwha, ururoa

Nearly 20% of a great white shark's brain is dedicated to its sense of smell. It can smell very faint odours from several kilometres away.

Sharks have a sixth sense that makes them extremely sensitive to the weak electrical fields that all animals produce. The electroreceptors, small pores dotted over its face, help a shark to focus on the fish or animal it is attacking. They might also help it navigate.

A white shark probably sees the world in black and white, but it has very good eyesight, both in and above water. There is a reflective layer at the back of its eyes, which helps it to see well, even in low light.

A white shark is an efficient swimmer, capable of short sprints as it chases prey, but it is more built for marathons – or even ultra-marathons. As it swims, much of its body stays stiff and streamlined, while its tail moves strongly from side to side, powered by a big mass of muscle along each flank.

The lateral line running from a shark's head along its sides is a series of sensory pores that enable the shark to be sensitive to changes in water pressure and to sense movements made by a fish or animal swimming nearby.

Lots of sharks are cold-blooded, but great whites have hot stomachs and hot muscles. They keep their internal body temperature between 24°C and 26°C. It makes them very efficient at digesting food and swimming.

A shark's skin is a suit of armour made of tiny scales. These are rough, like sandpaper, and they reduce the drag that's created as water flows across them. The scales are modified teeth, called dermal denticles, from the Latin word *dent*, meaning teeth.

This is what shark skin looks like when it's put under an electron microscope.

The shark featured on these pages is Alison, named after the author. She was 4 metres long when she was tagged with an acoustic tag at Stewart Island in 2011. The thin objects trailing from her fins are parasitic copepods, holding on with their strong mouths.

Who Are You?

Individual sharks have unique marks that are the shark equivalent of a human fingerprint. Most important are the patterns found around the gills, where grey pigment on the back of the shark meets the white of its belly.

Colour markings on the pelvic fins and tail are also very useful.

There are also distinctive cuts and notches on the trailing side of a shark's large dorsal fin.

Clinton Duffy has identified more than 170 sharks from Stewart Island, using photos taken from Kina's underwater camera. He has an uncanny ability to recognise a shark from a fleeting glimpse as it swims past the boat.

Caro is named after Kina Scollay's wife and she was 3.7 metres long when she was tagged with a SPOT tag at Stewart Island in 2014. She was tracked to Fiordland and the Auckland Islands, as well as the outer Great Barrier Reef. Her SPOT tag has become overgrown, but hasn't yet fallen off.

Chapter 3
Patting Sharks: Ella Goes North and South

Ella is one of the stars of the shark tagging programme. She was seen four years in a row at Stewart Island, beginning in 2008.

In autumn 2009, Ella was tagged with a PAT tag. She was 4 metres long. The tag showed that she swam to the Chesterfield Reefs in the Coral Sea, and she went there via the Great Barrier Reef in Australia.

Ella was the first tagged shark to go to the Chesterfield Reefs.

Since PAT tags were first used at the Chatham Islands in 2005, the team has seen a consistent pattern of New Zealand sharks making long-distance journeys to the tropics in winter. The sharks go to a wide range of places in the Pacific, from the Great Barrier Reef in the west, to as far east as Tonga. Only one shark, Kara, didn't go north.

However, none of the tagged Chatham Island great whites have ever gone to Stewart Island and vice versa, although the two populations overlap in Australia.

Malcolm and Clinton were keen to learn if sharks always returned to the same place in the Pacific and, to do this, they needed to tag individual sharks more than once.

They were very happy to see Ella again in 2010 and were able to tag her. Unfortunately, her tag came off after just five days. This wasn't unusual – disappointingly, a quarter of the PAT tags came off early, before the sharks had left New Zealand. Most likely the sharks rubbed against rocks and knocked their tags off, or other sharks could have bitten them off. Tags might also fail due to a flat battery or electrical malfunction.

When the team last saw Ella in 2011 she had grown to 4.4 metres. They tagged her

Ella was the first New Zealand white shark to be successfully tagged with a PAT tag in two different years, and the first to prove that some great whites return to the same place in the tropics each year.

again, and this time the PAT tag revealed important information. Ella *did* return to the Chesterfield Reefs – but she went via the Auckland Islands.

The subantarctic Auckland Islands are about 400 kilometres south of Stewart Island. Scientists used to think that the sea down there was too cold for sharks – in winter it's about 8°C at the surface, and just 3°C down deep.

But in April 1992, Mike Fraser was snorkelling on nearby Campbell Island when he was attacked by a great white shark. This was the first record of a white shark from the subantarctic, and it amazed the scientists. When Mike recovered, he became fascinated with white sharks and began searching for more records of them in the subantarctic. He found reports of New Zealand sea lions with large shark bites, and other scientists told him they even saw occasional white sharks near the big sea lion colony where they were working.

In 2007, a 4.4-metre-long white shark from Stewart Island named Kerri became the first tagged shark to be recorded in the subantarctic.

This is an important result from the tagging: finding out that New Zealand great white sharks go so far south and can spend many weeks in such cold water.

The breeding colonies of New Zealand sea lions in the subantarctic are a good source of food for a hungry shark. The female with the big bite mark on her back had a lucky escape.

Kerri is a record holder. During a deep dive near the Auckland Islands in August 2007 she set a world record low temperature for a great white shark of just 2.7°C. Then Kerri swam to Swain's Reef in Australia, where her tag recorded the hottest water temperature that a great white shark has ever reached: 26.6°C.

LOST AND FOUND

A quarter of the lost PAT tags were found and returned. This is amazing when you think how big the sea is and how small a tag is.

Each tag is a treasure trove of minute-by-minute data, so Malcolm and Clinton are always very keen to get them back. They pay a reward to people who find them.

After it pops up, a PAT tag signals where it is for up to 20 days, before its battery runs flat, so sometimes Malcolm and Clinton can ask people to go looking for it. A French shark scientist flew in by helicopter to hunt for Dave's tag on a remote beach in New Caledonia. A Department of Conservation ranger found a tag buried under a big pile of rotting kelp on the Chatham Islands. Malcolm rang up a tourist company that ran four-wheel drive tours along a beach in Queensland and asked them to look out for Marbletail's tag – and incredibly they managed to find it.

Tags can drift thousands of kilometres and still be found. A beachcomber in Queensland found Meca's tag, after it drifted there from New Caledonia. She wanted to keep it, so Malcolm persuaded her to swap that valuable tag for another from which the data had already been downloaded.

Roger Miller and other members of the Nuku'alofa Fishing Club searched for this tag, which had washed ashore on a reef off Tongatapu, the main island of Tonga. The tag came off Tim, a shark tagged at the Chatham Islands in 2008, and named after boat skipper Tim Gregory-Hunt.

HOW OLD IS THAT SHARK?

Sharks don't come with birth certificates, of course, so it's impossible to know exactly how old they are, but scientists use length (tip of nose to tip of tail) to group sharks into age categories.

Great white sharks grow fast when they are young, up to 30–50 centimetres a year. By the time they've grown to 2.6 metres long, they are about 6 years old.

They don't reach adulthood until they are about 10–15 years old, when their growth rate slows down.

Great white sharks live for a long time, with some surviving more than 70 years.

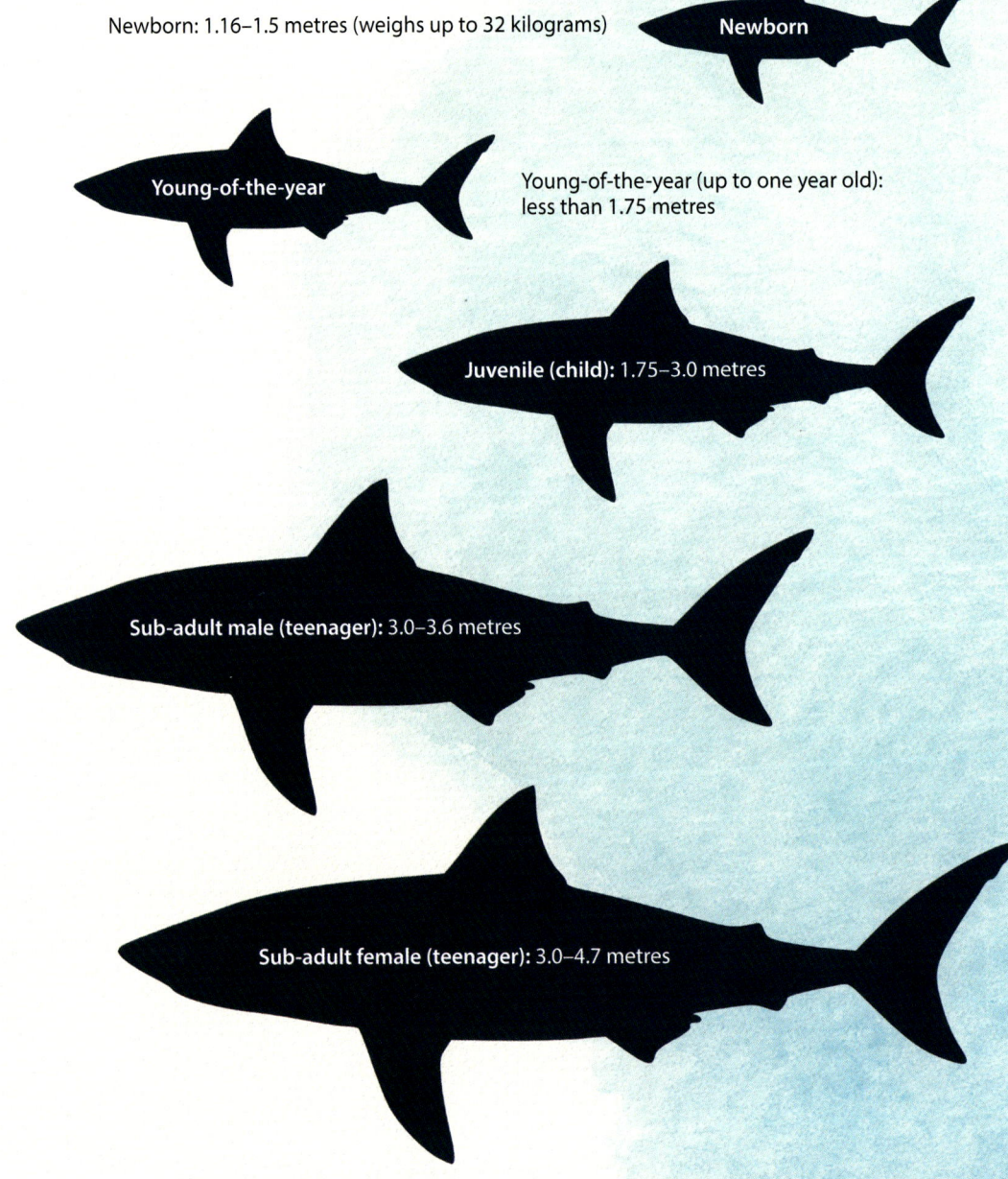

Newborn: 1.16–1.5 metres (weighs up to 32 kilograms) — Newborn

Young-of-the-year — Young-of-the-year (up to one year old): less than 1.75 metres

Juvenile (child): 1.75–3.0 metres

Sub-adult male (teenager): 3.0–3.6 metres

Sub-adult female (teenager): 3.0–4.7 metres

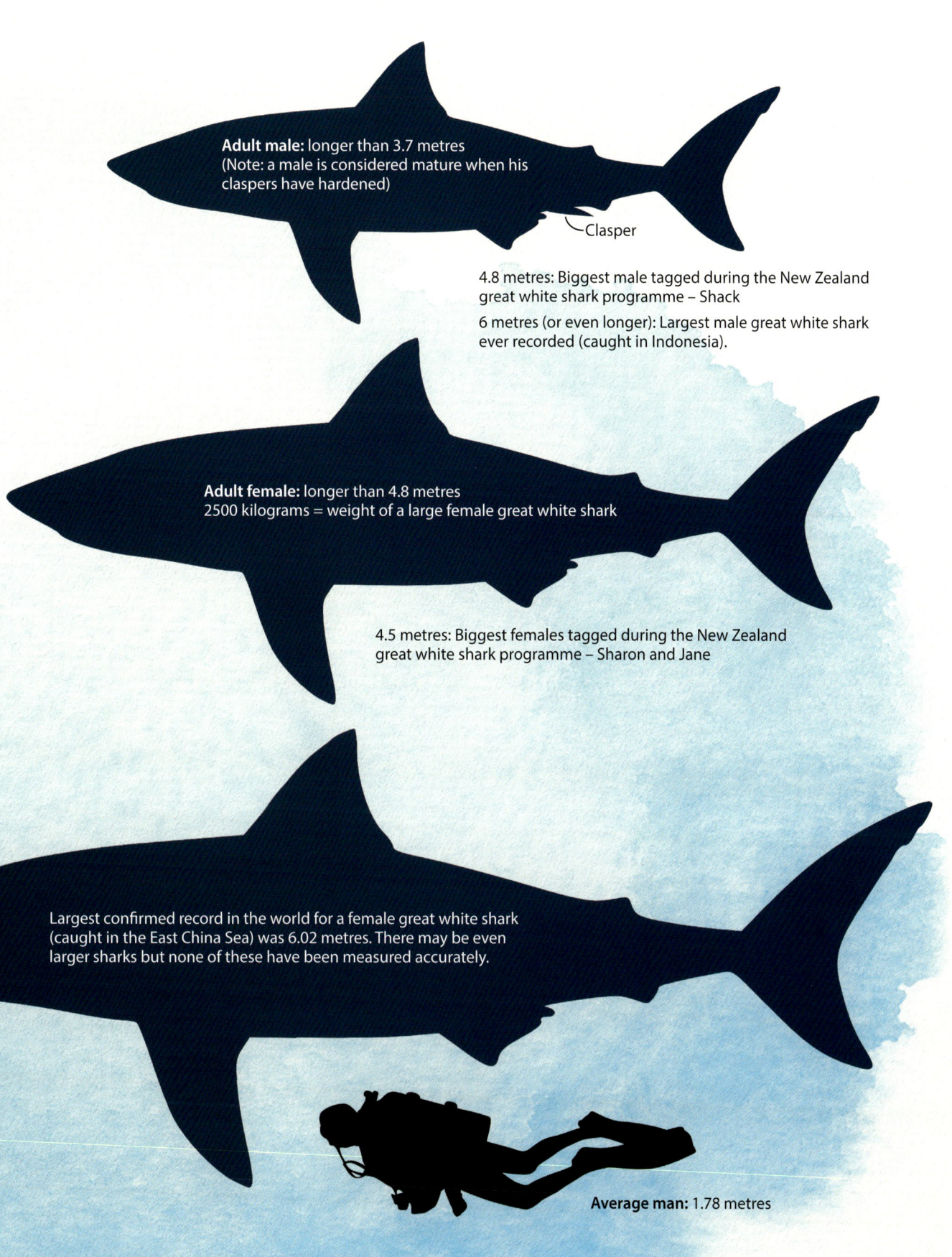

Chapter 4
LISTENING FOR SHARKS

Clinton and Malcolm wanted to find out the local movements of sharks around Stewart Island and in Foveaux Strait so, in 2011 and 2012, they put out 25 acoustic listening stations and they tagged 45 sharks with acoustic tags.

Each time a shark carrying an acoustic tag swims within 500 metres of an acoustic listening station, its identity and the date and time are recorded.

Each listening station is retrieved every three months so the data can be downloaded. They're hard to haul in, but luckily there's a hoist on the boat to do the heavy lifting.

Although they are marked by GPS co-ordinates and are attached to large, coloured buoys, this doesn't mean they are always easy to find amongst the big waves – and sometimes they just disappear.

Clinton Duffy with an acoustic listening station.

Fierce winds and storms funnel through Foveaux Strait, and the acoustic listening stations keep breaking free from their heavy anchors and drifting away in strong currents. Sharp shark teeth don't help. One buoy is bitten by a shark and sinks. Another buoy floats away after its rope is bitten through by a shark.

The acoustic tagging project ran for two-and-a-half years, and 18 acoustic listening stations were lost. But despite the problems, there are lots of interesting results.

During the four months or so that the sharks are at Stewart Island each year, they spend most of their time between 11 and 25 metres deep, and they hardly ever venture below 100 metres. The sea temperature is a cool 10–16°C.

Acoustic tracking also shows when sharks leave and return to Stewart Island. For three months after he is tagged, Nicholas Cage, like most of the other sharks with acoustic tags, is recorded frequently on the listening stations around Bench, North and Edwards islands, in the Titi Islands group. Some of the other listening stations get hardly any visitors. The Titi Islands are clearly a favourite spot.

By late July 2011 all the listening stations fall silent. The waters of Foveaux Strait are empty of sharks, and it stays that way for four months.

Then, in early December, a listening station at Stewart Island records a return visit – it is Nicholas Cage, back from who-knows-where, after his winter away? Over the next three months the sharks that haven't lost their acoustic tags gradually reappear, and by the time the project team turn up in March 2012 for their annual research trip, most of the sharks are back.

As usual, Clinton, Malcolm and Kina have two weeks to tag sharks and collect identification photos. They see some familiar faces plus a steady stream of new arrivals around the boat, but some sharks they know are missing.

There is no sign of Ella. The team thinks this is because she is nearly mature and has moved away from this coastal shark hotspot out into the open ocean.

Marbletail, with his acoustic tag clearly visible below his dorsal fin.

NICHOLAS CAGE EARNS HIS NAME

The team knows from the listening stations that Nicholas Cage has been around for three months, and he is often recorded at east Edwards Island where they are working. But they don't see him until day four of their trip – and he appears to be having an eventful summer. They're a little startled by how beaten-up he is. He has a 'necklace' of abrasions circling his head and neck.

It's only later that they piece together what they believe happened.

In February, the two regular shark-cage diving boats were already operating for the season. They take tourists diving with white sharks, from inside the safety of a metal cage.

That month, at Edwards Island, a shark tried to swim into a shark cage while divers were inside. The shark got stuck part way in, and the divers escaped to safety out the top of the cage. The shark eventually wrestled itself free.

When Malcolm and Clinton take a closer look at the data from the listening station at the island, they notice that Nicholas Cage was present on the day the shark cage incident happened, and his scars

Phred approaches a shark cage off Edwards Island, near Stewart Island.

are consistent with those a shark would receive forcing its way in – and then out of – a metal cage. They conclude that he was most likely that shark.

So that's how Nicholas Cage got his nickname: firstly 'Cage', and then 'Nicholas', to match the name of a famous Hollywood actor.

The Stewart Island Shark Gang

Nicholas Cage is a typical member of the Stewart Island shark gang. He's a young male, big enough to hunt seals, but not old enough to be seriously interested in girls.

Boys in the gang outnumber girls by more than two to one. Almost all the girls and most of the boys are teenagers. The rest of the males are adults.

There are some unwritten rules amongst the sharks in the gang. The main one is that size matters in the shark world. If you're a small shark, you give way to a big shark. If you don't, you'll probably get bitten. Girls tend to grow much bigger than the boys, so this pretty much means girls have right of way.

Adult sharks have sex on their mind. This is when they leave the gang and the coast to head out to the open sea.

Scientists in Australia have a network of permanent listening stations around the Australian coast. Meadsy, a 2.8-metre male shark tagged with an acoustic tag at Stewart Island, was detected on Sydney's Bondi Line of acoustic listening stations for two years in a row. Emer, a 2.5-metre female, was one of the smallest sharks seen at Stewart Island; she and Bruce were also detected on listening stations in Australia, while a small unnamed male was detected at the Chesterfield Reefs.

Marbletail is named for the unusual white marbled patterns on his tail. He has the record for being the most tagged shark. In 2011, when he was 3.5 metres long, he was tagged with an acoustic tag that came off. In 2012, he was tagged with both an acoustic and a PAT tag at the same time, earning him the nickname 'Bling Boy' for wearing so much 'jewellery'. This PAT tag also came off early.

In 2014, when Marbletail had grown to 4 metres long, he was tagged again with a PAT tag, and he went via the subantarctic Auckland Islands to Fraser Island, at the southern end of the Great Barrier Reef. In this photo his large claspers are visible.

Great whites have 24 lower teeth and 26 upper teeth. Behind these, there are five rows of developing teeth that are ready to rotate into place if a tooth gets broken or falls out.

Snapper

ON THE MENU

Great white sharks eat all kinds of food.

Kids' menu: Small great whites have narrow grasping teeth, perfect for biting fish and other smaller sharks. They're fast for their age and able to chase down fish.

Hungry, growing teens: By the time they're about 2.5–3 metres long, great white sharks are getting stronger. They lose their baby fish-eating teeth and get adult teeth that are wider and serrated, designed to cut flesh. They're also big enough to tackle small seals and dolphins.

Grown-ups: Once a great white shark reaches full size, at more than 4 metres long, it can hunt almost anything but, while a big shark can eat big prey, it might also choose to eat lots of a small prey. Mature sharks don't spend so much time at the coast. They live and feed in the open ocean, where there are plenty of squid to add their main diet of fish and sharks.

The amount of energy required by a great white shark the size of Nicholas Cage is equivalent to eating a seal pup every three days, or a 4.5-kilogram fish every day. A sub-adult male white shark in South Africa was found with six young seals in its stomach.

If there is a dead whale, great white sharks waste no time in eating as much energy-rich blubber as they can fit in. Kilo-for-kilo, whale blubber contains about three times as much energy as a seal pup.

White sharks sometimes eat unusual things. Retired Otago Museum curator John Darby carried out an autopsy on a large dead female white shark found in Otago Harbour in the 1960s. As well as a few marine snails, she had a whole crayfish pot in her stomach. It was a bit bent out of shape!

Squid

Fur seal

Chapter 5
SHARK SPOTTING

March, 2013: Malcolm and Clinton head to Stewart Island, and they're going to be busy. They require more underwater video footage for the shark identification project, they want to collect tiny samples of tissue from sharks so they can look at their genetics, and they're using SPOT tags this time.

SPOT tags on sharks are a much bigger challenge for the team. The tag is attached to a shark's dorsal fin – and the team needs to *catch* the shark, rather than have it just swim past the back of the boat.

It must be a small- to medium-sized shark, as large sharks are too heavy to catch. And it must be on its own, because other sharks could bite it while it is restrained.

Clinton will have to hook the shark through the side of its jaw. This is so they can manoeuvre it along the side of the boat where there's a small gate. And the boat can't be at anchor but must be kept slowly moving forward so water is always moving over the shark's gills.

With all this in mind, it's time to go fishing.

They put out the berley. After several hours a shark turns up. He circles enthusiastically around the bait a few times allowing for lots of good underwater footage. He takes the baited hook but he's big and strong and, just as they're getting him alongside the boat, he powers away. The curved fishing hook pulls straight and slips out.

The team move to another location but after a few more hours of berleying and no sharks seen it's time to head home for the night.

The next morning there are more hours of berleying with no sharks to show for it.

At a different site in the afternoon there are suddenly too many sharks around the boat. The team manage to get tissue samples from two of them. To do this, they aim at the shark's back but, instead of darting a tag in, they use a sharp tip on the end of the long tagging pole, which cuts out a small piece of skin and tissue.

The following day is another frustrating one. In the morning, the only shark that appears is a large female, too big to try and tag. And a male in the afternoon is too wary and doesn't come close enough.

Tagging sharks is a long, slow process! Clinton and Malcolm are worried that they're running out of time.

To try and limit how many sharks turn up, they decide not to use berley, just the tuna bait.

It works. Finally. They are at west Edwards Island, and mid-morning a familiar shark turns up. It's Nicholas Cage. He's keen on the bait and in a co-operative mood. Not only this, but the weather conditions are perfect – the sea is calm and there's very little wind. They'll have to work as quickly as possible so the shark can be tagged and freed without getting too stressed.

Nicholas Cage takes the baited hook and immediately speeds away, going with the current. The hook is attached to a steel trace and then to a rope, which is tied to buoys. The buoys float on the surface, making it harder for the shark to dive down. Three people grab the rope and begin to slowly move Nic towards the boat. He tries to stay deep but the combined efforts of the men and the buoys keep him rising towards the surface.

Nicholas Cage takes the baited hook.

It takes 25 minutes to tire Nic out and get him alongside the boat. Clinton grabs the steel trace – he has to keep the shark's head up out of the water so that it planes smoothly beside the moving boat. Even though Nic is quiet and not fighting, it's still hard work.

Once Nic is in position, they must lasso a rope around his head. Twice he manages to grab the rope in his mouth and they have to cut the rope free. On the third attempt they succeed, sliding the rope down to sit around his middle. They tie another rope around his tail.

With Nic secure, and water moving across his gills so that he can breathe, it's time for Malcolm to get to work. He lies on his stomach on the deck and leans out the small open door in the side of the boat towards Nic's big dorsal fin.

In one hand Malcolm has a template marked with three holes and in the other a cordless drill. He holds the template up against the left-hand side of Nic's dorsal fin and begins to drill three small holes, one near the top of the fin and two below. Nic remains calm as Malcolm holds the SPOT tag up against his fin and slips the three protruding bolts through the holes.

Now the hard part begins. Malcolm has to reach around to the other side of Nic's fin and tighten a nut to the end of each bolt. This is tricky. He is at full stretch, and as he can't see anything, he's got to do it by feel. And until he fits the first nut, there's a risk he might drop the tag in the sea. Malcolm gets the first nut on. Everyone stops holding their breath. Then the second and third nuts are in place. It's done.

Just before they release Nic, they quickly

run a tape measure from the tip of his nose to the tip of his tail: 3.51 metres. He's grown about 70 centimetres in the past two years.

They cut the rope around his tail and then the one around his chest. Clinton is still holding onto the trace, making sure the shark stays upright. Then the last task: cutting through the fishing hook with a pair of bolt cutters. Nic is free. He sinks for a second, then turns onto his right side and cruises away into the depths.

Malcolm looks at his watch. 11.53am. The whole process has taken 51 minutes, but it feels much longer.

The team head out for a few more days but they have no more luck with tagging. They don't see Nic again and neither do they get any pings from his tag. They're concerned but it may be that he's just not coming to the surface. Unless the tag comes out of the water, it can't send a signal.

Finally, two weeks later, one of the shark-cage diving boat operators sends a photo of Nic's tagged fin. It was taken near his dive boat at east Edwards Island – he's alive and well.

Soon after, Nic starts transmitting and sending regular updates of his travels around Foveaux Strait. The SPOT tag is a success.

Phred was first tagged with a PAT tag in 2009, and tracked to the Chesterfield Reefs. In 2012 – at least 4.5 metres long, and one of the largest sharks recorded at Stewart Island – he was seen and tagged again. Unfortunately, this tag came off early. He was sighted again in 2013, 2014 and 2016; no other shark has been seen over so many years. He is named after Department of Conservation ranger Phred Dobbins, who often helped with shark tagging. In this photo, he's being escorted by a small pilot fish.

BUILT FOR THE KILL

Great white sharks use all their senses when hunting for prey:

- Sense of smell: A shark can detect and track its prey from several kilometres away.
- Sight and feel: As a shark gets closer to its prey, it can see what it's aiming for and it feels the movements that a swimming or struggling animal is making.
- Taste: A shark uses its mouth the way we use our hands. It has super-sensitive teeth, a jawbone that's also filled with nerves, and a mouth full of taste buds. As it bites down on something, a shark can sense whether it will be a tasty dinner or something that it should spit out.

Great white sharks have excellent hunting tactics:

- A shark often attacks from down low. Its dark back camouflages it against the sea floor.
- If a shark approaches its prey at the water's surface, it may attack out of the sun. A seal, for example, looking towards the sun will be dazzled by the brightness and is less likely to see the shark.
- As it closes in for the kill, a shark rolls its eyes backwards into the eye sockets for protection.
- In the final seconds before a shark bites, its top jaw juts forward, putting its teeth in the best position to attack.
- A great white shark can accelerate very quickly for short periods of time.
- A shark can launch itself up out of the water and be completely airborne.

The shark opposite has shot its top jaw forward as it comes in to bite.

Chapter 6
AN OCEAN JOURNEY

In late June 2013, about seven weeks after he was tagged with a SPOT tag, Nicholas Cage begins his journey to the Pacific. He leaves Stewart Island and heads around the southwest corner of New Zealand past Fiordland. The great white shark team monitor his progress.

From: Malcolm Francis, NIWA
To: Clinton Duffy, Kina Scollay
Sent: 10 July 2013
Subject: Tracking Nicholas Cage

Nic has now steamed up the west side of NZ. His track has been amazingly straight – he clearly knows how to hold a course. Most of the fixes have been in the afternoon/evening, though last night we got some fixes scattered through the night.

This means Nicholas Cage is coming to the surface each afternoon and evening, and his SPOT tag is out of the water. For the rest of the time he is in deeper water.

From: Malcolm Francis, NIWA
To: Clinton Duffy, Kina Scollay
Sent: 19 July 2013
Subject: Re tracking Nicholas Cage

After heading in a straight line for many days (aimed at about Fiji), he has turned west and is now heading towards New Caledonia. Looks like he'll make the trip in about 3 weeks – he's doing 130 km per day.

One hundred and thirty kilometres a day is an average speed of 5.4 kilometres an hour. It doesn't sound like much – but, then again, imagine walking non-stop for three weeks. Of course if Nicholas Cage, or any other white shark, did actually stop moving they'd die. They need to have water moving across their gills at all times.

What is Nicholas Cage doing during his long ocean journey? When he leaves Stewart Island, Nic swims just above the sea floor, staying over the shallow continental shelf as he heads out of Foveaux Strait and around into Fiordland. Then, as he reaches open sea, the continental shelf falls away steeply beneath him to the ocean floor 4 kilometres below.

His behaviour changes and he begins to make lots of deep dives. For two-thirds of the time he swims right at the surface, in the top metre of water. Twenty per cent of the time he's between 200 and 800 metres, and on rare occasions he dives deeper than 1000 metres.

He usually starts his deep dives at dawn and at night. His dives last between one and four hours, but occasionally he stays down for more than 12 hours, and on one occasion he dives for more than 24 hours before surfacing.

The sea floor beneath Nic is complex, covered with steep canyons and tall mountains. At times it is several kilometres below him, and at other times he can easily dive down and reach it.

On 23 July, after nearly four weeks swimming more than 3000 kilometres, Nicholas Cage reaches the deep seas around the island of Lifou, to the east of New Caledonia. Even though Nic is not in shallow coastal waters, Malcolm decides to alert the local authorities. There is a front-page story in the local newspaper, but despite lots of interest and some concerns from Lifou residents there is no sign of Nicholas Cage.

Even the scientists lose touch with him. Malcolm worries that Nic might have been caught by a fishing boat but, more likely, he's just staying down below the surface. In mid-October a single location has him over deep water between Lifou and New Caledonia.

Then, silence.

HOW SHARKS NAVIGATE

How does Nicholas Cage find his way across thousands of kilometres of ocean? This is one of the great shark mysteries.

Moving up and down the coast, like most of Australia's sharks do, is simple – keep the land on one side as you swim north, and on the other side as you swim south.

Out in the open ocean it's much trickier. There are several possibilities and, who knows, Nicholas may be using some or even all of them.

Some animals use a sun compass or steer by the stars. He's certainly able to see the sky when he's near the surface of the ocean.

He could be following the earth's magnetic field lines, which extend between the north and south magnetic poles. We use the earth's magnetic field when we use a compass, and some animals seem to have an in-built compass that allows them to do the same.

We often use familiar landmarks to help us find our way around, and there are features on the ocean floor that might help sharks: long undersea ridges, the edge of the continental shelf, sea mounts and canyons. The depth of the ocean might be another clue. Perhaps that's why Nicholas Cage keeps diving as he travels – to find these underwater landmarks.

His other senses might also help. The ocean is filled with different masses of water and currents that can be different temperatures. Sharks have such a good sense of smell that maybe they can smell different water masses. And maybe sound helps as well.

Sharks sense the world so differently to us that it's hard to imagine what they're experiencing. But however they do it, the end result is that they can swim in incredibly straight lines over thousands of kilometres. And some sharks seem able to retrace the same route, year after year.

What's the Tropical Attraction?

Why do New Zealand great white sharks swim thousands of kilometres to the tropics for winter and spring? Many of the migrating sharks are immature, so breeding isn't the answer.

Food seems to be the main attraction.

Sharks might be following humpback whales. In autumn, humpback whales migrate past New Zealand on their way to New Caledonia, Tonga, Niue and the Cook Islands to breed. More humpback whales migrate up the east coast of Australia. They spend the winter in the tropics and then head back south in spring. There could be dead whales along the way, as well as vulnerable young calves and afterbirth.

But there are other reasons apart from following whales. There's certainly plenty of easy food for sharks in the tropics, especially tuna, which is a favourite shark food. The white sharks are also there when lots of reef fish and deep-sea fish gather in enormous schools for breeding. In deeper water they probably feed on squid.

Even though great white sharks are able to stay warm in cold water, perhaps the warmth of the tropics is an attraction, especially for smaller sharks.

In October 2015, a research team tagging humpback whales at Raoul Island, in the Kermadecs, spotted a dead whale calf floating on the sea surface. They headed over to investigate and found a 4-metre great white shark feeding on it. From this photo, Clinton recognised this unnamed male from Stewart Island. STWI1009 was first identified at Edwards Island, in March 2010, when he was about 2.8 metres long. In 2011 the team tagged him with an acoustic tag. He left Stewart Island in June, and turned up four months later on a listening station at the Chesterfield Reefs, in the Coral Sea. He wasn't seen again at Stewart Island but here he was, four years later, at the Kermadecs.

In 2010, a 2.8-metre shark called Dave, one of the smallest sharks seen at Stewart Island, set a world record of 1246 metres for the deepest dive ever made by a great white shark. He was on his way to New Caledonia.

Diving Deep

Why do great white sharks dive so deep? There must be something pretty good down there to make the effort of swimming back up again worthwhile.

They are probably hunting. There are lots of deep-sea fishes and squid down there, including giant squid. The sharks dive down so deep that it is completely dark, but that won't matter to them. Many deep-sea fish have lights or they glow in the dark. And anyway, great whites only hunt by sight when they are very close to their prey. They mostly find food by smell and by detecting electrical fields given off by other animals. And in the dark they can sneak up on things.

There is an interesting layer of water between 600 and 1200 metres deep called the Sound Fixing and Ranging (SOFAR) channel. This allows underwater sounds, such as whale calls, to travel hundreds of kilometres. Could the sharks be following these sounds?

WHERE IN THE WORLD

Great white sharks live in most parts of the Pacific, Atlantic and Indian oceans. Well-studied great white shark populations occur on the east and west coasts of North America, South Africa, Australia and New Zealand.

Not much is known about them, but great whites are also found off the coasts of Chile and Brazil in South America, in the Mediterranean Sea, around Japan and Taiwan, and several very big white sharks have been caught in Asia, including one very close to the Equator. There are no records of great whites crossing the Equator.

In Africa, white sharks are found mostly in cool coastal waters, but they are occasionally recorded in warmer waters as far north as Kenya, around Indian Ocean islands such as Mauritius and Madagascar, as well as in cold water around subantarctic Marion Island. A sub-adult female, Nicole, famously swam all the way across the Indian Ocean to western Australia, and back again. There is one record of a mature female caught at remote Gough Island in the middle of the Atlantic Ocean.

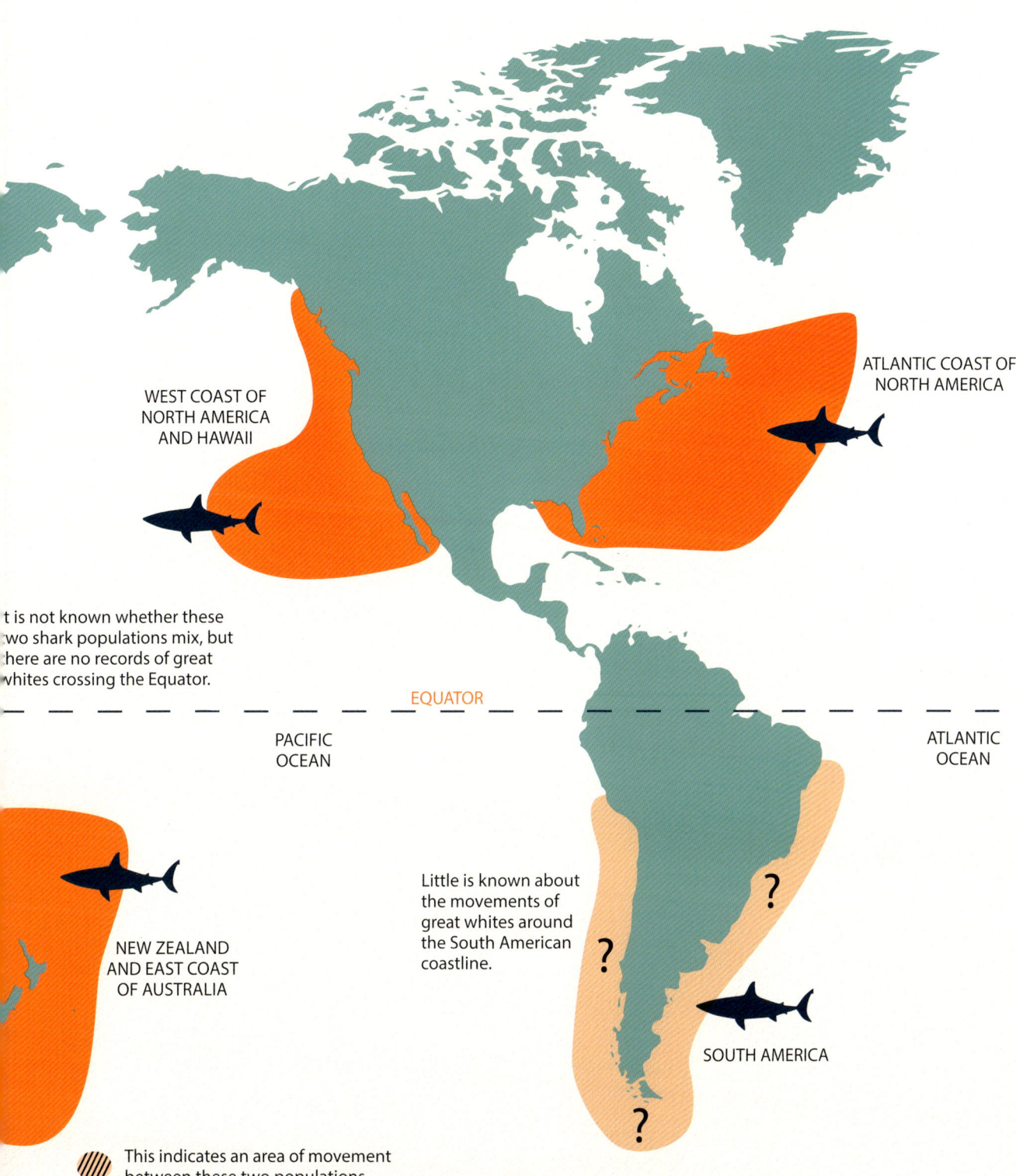

WEST COAST OF NORTH AMERICA AND HAWAII

ATLANTIC COAST OF NORTH AMERICA

It is not known whether these two shark populations mix, but there are no records of great whites crossing the Equator.

EQUATOR

PACIFIC OCEAN

ATLANTIC OCEAN

NEW ZEALAND AND EAST COAST OF AUSTRALIA

Little is known about the movements of great whites around the South American coastline.

SOUTH AMERICA

This indicates an area of movement between these two populations.

Adult white sharks in the eastern Pacific Ocean, from California and Mexico, trek out to sea every year, either to Hawaii or a large area out in the middle of nowhere. This area has been called the Shared Offshore Foraging Area, or SOFA, and also the Shark Café (it's thought they eat a lot of squid while they are there).

In the western Atlantic Ocean, white sharks move up and down the coast of North America, from Florida north to Newfoundland, and east as far as Bermuda. Some big females have been tagged there recently, and they are constantly on the move and spend a lot of time out at sea.

Chapter 7
HEADING HOME

From: Malcolm Francis, NIWA
To: Clinton Duffy, Kina Scollay
Sent: 15 December 2013
Subject: Nicholas Cage checks in

Nic has checked in due east of Norfolk Island, presumably on his way home. We've had six other messages without locations in the last week, so he has probably been migrating for a while. But perhaps the tag is fouled and not talking to the satellite very well.

Nicholas Cage's journey back to New Zealand follows the same general direction as his northward swim, but he's not retracing his exact route – this time he is quite a bit further west. He's still a long way offshore and drawing level with Westport when he suddenly turns and begins to swim north again.

Offshore from Auckland he stops. Malcolm and Clinton wonder what the attraction might be. At 3.5 metres long, Nicholas Cage is nearly an adult, and perhaps this is where adult sharks meet. Is he just checking it out? Or has he sniffed a dead whale carcass? They don't know.

After a few days he turns around and heads back down the west coast, following the edge of the narrow continental shelf on almost exactly the same route he went north on.

His tag is sending only a few messages, but he seems to be dawdling on his way back, and making a few detours. It's not until early February that Nic's tag finally reports in from Stewart Island.

NICHOLAS CAGE TRACKING MAP 2013-14

Nicholas Cage swam more than 8900 kilometres, to the tropics and back, covering about 130 kilometres each day.

From: Malcolm Francis, NIWA
To: Clinton Duffy, Kina Scollay
Sent: 7 February 2014
Subject: NC at Stewart Island

Shark-cage dive operator Peter Scott has seen Nicholas Cage at Edwards Island over the last two days. He looks in great condition but the tag is lying horizontally so no wonder we haven't been getting great fixes from him. Apparently he is grabbing all their bait.

Because Nicholas Cage's tag is loose, it means the aerial is often pointing backwards rather than upwards toward satellites. This explains why he has been sending irregular signals. It's not good news, but it's heartening to hear he's in good form after his long journey – over 8900 kilometres, from Stewart Island to New Caledonia and back, with a detour up to Auckland.

But there's trouble brewing. Stewart Island locals are worried that the shark-cage dive operations are encouraging more sharks to stay around and teaching them to associate humans and boats with food. The shark-cage dive operators claim that the white sharks are there because of the seals, and not because of them. Tensions are high and not everyone is happy that the great whites are back at the island.

On 13 February, Nic's tag sends a single ping with no location; it's the first message in six days. Then, nothing.

Sadly, this is the last time anyone ever hears from – or sees – Nicholas Cage.

Malcolm and Clinton begin to receive reports that earlier in the week a Stewart Island fisher set a net to catch butterfish at the known shark hotspot of west Edwards Island, where the shark-cage dive boats often operate. The fisher tells a visiting TV crew, 'The shark got caught in my net and it died and I let it go.'

The great white shark is protected in New Zealand waters and it is illegal to deliberately kill one. Fishers have to let the Department of Conservation know if they accidentally catch a great white shark. If it is alive they have to let it go unharmed, and if it is dead they have to discard it at sea.

Was this shark Nicholas Cage? The fisher says he didn't see a tag, but the loose tag could have been knocked off as the shark struggled in the net or the fisher may have only seen the animal on the side away from the tag.

Is it just a coincidence that Nicholas Cage, usually a bold and curious shark around the shark-cage dive boats and the research boat, is never seen again? We'll only know if he's still alive when someone positively identifies him.

GREAT WHITE SHARK ATTACKS

Sharks are always big news, and it's easy to get the impression that great whites are lurking everywhere waiting to attack. But what do the official numbers say?

The International Shark Attack File (ISAF) keeps records of attacks by all sorts of sharks from around the world. It distinguishes between unprovoked attacks and provoked attacks. Provoked attacks are when people are doing something that attract sharks, such as spear fishing and having bleeding fish in the water, and ISAF doesn't count these.

In 2015, ISAF confirmed that there were 98 unprovoked shark attacks, worldwide, six of which were fatal. Remember this is out of 7.4 billion people living on the planet! And great white sharks are not the only sharks that attack people.

Since 1852 there have been 49 unprovoked shark attacks in New Zealand, eight of which were fatal. A fatal shark attack occurs about once every 13 years.

By comparison, about 100 people drown in New Zealand each year, so you are far more likely to drown than be mauled by a shark.

Shack, named after Kina Scollay's son, was the largest adult male shark tagged in New Zealand. In 2009, when he was first seen at Stewart Island, he was estimated to be 4.8 metres long. He was tagged with a PAT tag and went to the Great Barrier Reef. He was seen again at Stewart Island by a shark-cage dive boat, six years later, in 2015.

Chapter 8
THE AUSTRALIAN CONNECTION

TRACKING PIP

From: Malcolm Francis, NIWA
To: Kina Scollay
Sent: 30 March 2014
Subject: Pip

Great day — we SPOT tagged a 3.3-metre female after a lot of effort. She took off pretty well so we think she is okay.

The month after Nicholas Cage disappears, Clinton and Malcolm attach a SPOT tag to a female great white shark at Stewart Island. They name her Pip.

They don't hear from Pip for nearly three months, and they assume that she is just getting on with local shark business and not coming to the surface.

When her SPOT tag sends its first report in late June they're pleased to hear that she's still alive, and they think she must be on her way north. But instead she heads south, into cold deep water. Then she heads back to Stewart Island, changes her mind and goes south again. Finally, she decides to swim north.

From: Malcolm Francis, NIWA
To: Clinton Duffy, Kina Scollay
Sent: 30 July 2014
Subject: Halfway

```
Pip is now more than halfway across the Tasman, aiming at southern New South Wales. She
has also settled into a pattern of coming up to the surface in the afternoons, usually between
2-8pm, but sometimes later.
```

A week later, Pip arrives near Sydney, on the Australian coast. Her 2020-kilometre trans-Tasman commute has taken her 20 days. Her average swimming speed is a slow but steady 4.2 kilometres an hour, just a bit slower than Nicholas Cage.

Pip begins to make her way north from Sydney, hugging the coastline. After a couple of days she finds herself at Hawks Nest, which is one of Australia's most well-known great white shark hotspots.

THE AUSTRALIAN GREAT WHITE SHARK PROJECT

Quite a few tagged Stewart Island sharks have travelled to the east coast of Australia, which has its own well-studied population of great white sharks.

The Australian great white shark project has tagged more than 300 sharks with electronic tags. One of the important discoveries has been that Australia has two, quite separate, populations of white sharks: one on the east coast and one on the west coast.

Almost all the tagged sharks stayed in Australian waters. That is probably because Australia is so big that sharks can move from cool southern waters to warm tropical water just by swimming up the coast.

Barry Bruce is an Australian biologist who has studied great white sharks all around Australia since 1987. He works for Australia's science organisation CSIRO, and he leads a team of shark experts from different government departments and universities. Barry has tagged many great white sharks and says he is always awe-struck by them, even the small ones.

Most east coast sharks swim up and down from Tasmania and Victoria to New South Wales and Queensland. Sharks in the western population, on the other hand, mainly swim from Victoria and South Australia around to Western Australia.

AUSTRALIA'S SHARK NURSERIES

Hawks Nest is a popular surf beach on the New South Wales coast, and lots of great white sharks hang out just at the back of the surf break, and sometimes even in it, in water that's just 1–5 metres deep.

The sharks here are almost all juveniles, between 1.7–2.6 metres long and aged between two and six years old. As well as staying out of the way of bigger sharks that would eat them, the juvenile sharks are definitely here for the fish.

From a boat or a small plane it's very easy to see the sharks, as they stand out clearly in the clear water against the white sandy bottom. Because of this it's a good place for Barry Bruce and his colleagues to count and tag them, and they have become world experts on juvenile great white sharks.

The sharks are here in big numbers. At peak shark time, scientists have estimated there are up to 250 young great whites.

Hawks Nest is part of a large nursery area that is centred around Port Stephens.

It is one of two white shark nurseries that Barry and his team have found. The other nursery is in southeast Victoria, along Ninety Mile Beach near Corner Inlet. Both nurseries are long surf beaches, next to large estuaries.

The young sharks come and go from the Port Stephens nursery at any time of year, but they're most common in spring and summer. On average, they hang out here for two to three months. They don't spend all of their time in the surf – most of the time they're over the nearby continental shelf where the water is up to 120 metres deep. They split their time between the top five metres of water, and depths of 60 to 100 metres.

When they leave the Port Stephens nursery the young Australian sharks may range along 2000 kilometres of coast, as far north as the southern Great Barrier Reef and south to waters around Tasmania.

During summer and autumn many of the sharks end up 850 kilometres away from Port Stephens, in the Ninety Mile Beach nursery. Then, in late autumn and winter, they head north again, back to northern New South Wales and Queensland, returning to Port Stephens by spring.

When Pip passes through Port Stephens in mid-winter there wouldn't have been many other sharks around. Perhaps that is why she doesn't stick around, but carries on up to the Great Barrier Reef.

The little sharks don't always hug the coast. Some of the tagged juveniles have swum out into open ocean, and what's amazing is that when they're out over deep water these little sharks can also dive to 1000 metres deep, just like the big sharks.

Two young sharks tagged at the Port Stephens nursery even swam to New Zealand. One of these was a 2.1-metre male, who is the smallest great white known to have made this long ocean trip.

Barry and the Australian great white shark project have found out a lot about the behaviour and movements of small white sharks, but they still have lots of questions, such as 'where are Australian sharks born?' Barry doesn't have proof, yet, but he thinks that eastern Bass Strait is a pupping area for east coast white sharks.

Another intriguing question is how closely related are the New Zealand and Australian sharks – are they one big family, or are they just friendly neighbours who like visiting?

NEW ZEALAND'S YOUNG SHARKS

Clinton has been trying to tag juvenile white sharks in New Zealand. He does find them, but he hasn't found a place that might be a white shark pupping area or a nursery area, and he thinks that breeding happens over a wide area.

His archive of white shark records shows that young-of-the-year sharks and small juveniles up to 2.5 metres long are most common around Auckland and Northland.

Many of the very young great white sharks are recorded in places such as the Kaipara and Manukau harbours, near Auckland. The water there is warm and shallow but, unfortunately, these harbours are also muddy, so it's very difficult to find sharks there.

Clinton has seen a newborn shark, just 1.5 metres long, in the Kaipara Harbour. He says this suggests that New Zealand female sharks give birth around the upper North Island rather than in the tropics, as little sharks don't make long trips until they are more than 2 metres long.

How DNA Can Help Us Understand White Sharks

The DNA in a tiny sample of skin and muscle from a great white shark can tell scientists a lot. It can help work out how individual sharks are related to one another. It can help identify how populations of great white sharks in different countries are related to one another. And it can also help work out how many sharks there are in each population.

One of the most important things that DNA research has shown so far is that pregnant female white sharks give birth in the same place that they were born.

Let's take a great white shark that was born around northern New Zealand, for example. When she's big and old enough she'll move from there and begin spending time at Stewart Island and in Australia. But when she's pregnant and about to give birth, she will go back to northern New Zealand.

When her daughters get pregnant they will also go back to their birthplace in northern New Zealand to have their babies.

Scientists now think that most male great white sharks also return to their birthplace to breed.

The tiny bits of DNA collected from different individuals can also tell us how sharks in different parts of the world are related. Great white sharks in New Zealand are most closely related to those in Australia, but only distantly related to other white sharks in the Pacific Ocean, such as those in Japan and California.

Interestingly, sharks from east Australia mix with, and are related to, those from New Zealand, but sharks from the west and east of Australia are genetically quite distinct from each other.

There are some surprises in this story: a few sharks with South African DNA have been found in east Australia. One possible explanation is that occasionally a female from South Africa swims to Australia and stays there to give birth.

And while you'd think that white sharks in the Mediterranean Sea would be most closely related to white sharks in the Atlantic Ocean, it turns out their closest cousins are from the Pacific, including New Zealand.

Chapter 9
MOTHERS AND BABIES

After spending three months at the southern end of the Great Barrier Reef, in mid-December, Pip begins her journey back to New Zealand. Her return journey follows exactly the same angle as her inbound course, but offset about 100 kilometres to the north.

Pip's migration has taken her on a 9500-kilometre journey, but by late January 2015 she is well and truly back home in the Titi Islands. She sinks off the radar again, lurking beneath the surface, getting on with teenage shark business.

Pip is still part of the Stewart Island shark gang but, just like Ella and the other bigger girls have done, she'll move away as she nears adulthood. And while Australian scientists such as Barry have discovered much about young sharks, and Malcolm and Clinton have learnt lots about the teenagers, what adult sharks do – and where they do it – is still a mystery.

SHARK SEX

No one has ever seen great white sharks having sex. This is because there are not many great white sharks, sex takes place underwater, and mature female sharks spend most of their time out at sea, and we still don't know where.

Based on what happens with other kinds of sharks, scientists do know that great white shark sex will be rough. The male approaches the larger female from behind. He bites her around her pectoral fin or head to hold on as he tries to wrestle himself around so he can face her belly-to-belly. He needs to subdue her long enough to get one of his claspers into her cloaca, and then use seawater to pump his sperm into her. (Claspers work a bit like a water pistol.)

As a result of the biting, adult female great white sharks often have large wounds around their fins and gills. When scientists

see a female with fresh bite marks they know she has mated recently. Luckily sharks heal quickly.

Great white sharks don't pair up with one another, they just meet to mate.

Shark scientists think there are breeding grounds where adult white sharks meet up at certain times of the year but, for now, they have no idea where New Zealand's or Australia's great whites go to breed.

PREGNANT GREAT WHITES

Pregnant great white sharks are another big mystery, and much of what we know comes from just one female shark from New Zealand.

In 1991, Malcolm heard about a pregnant white shark that had been caught in a set net in shallow water at North Cape and had unfortunately died. Until 1991 there had been fewer than six reports, worldwide, of pregnant white sharks and their embryos, and no scientist had ever examined one.

The fishers brought the 5.36-metre shark back to shore and cut her up for bait. They kept the jaws and gave two of her seven embryos to a taxidermist. Everything else was thrown off the wharf.

It was more than six weeks before Malcolm could get there, but he was determined to dive around the wharf just in case he could find something. He describes it as a horrible dive: he couldn't see anything in the shallow muddy water, so he was feeling his way around rubbish in the hope of stumbling across something.

His persistence paid off when he found a single large vertebra. The dark, smelly mud had stained the vertebra, revealing 22

In 2003, a 5.5-metre pregnant white shark accidentally drowned in a fishing net in the Hauraki Gulf. When the fishers towed her ashore they discovered she was pregnant with three pups. The pups were still alive and they held them in the water until they swam away. By the time Clinton and Malcolm heard the news it was too late to investigate. She was only the second pregnant white shark recorded in New Zealand.

distinct black and white bands. This meant the female was at least 22 years old. Young sharks produce annual growth rings in their vertebra, just like a tree adds a new ring to its trunk every year.

Malcolm was also able to study the two frozen embryos, and from all the information he'd gathered, he wrote an important summary about white shark reproduction. Malcolm presented this to other scientists at the second international white shark conference in 1993, where a team of Japanese scientists also reported on two pregnant white sharks caught near Japan. Not much more has been discovered since then, and shark scientists around the world still rely on Malcolm's research.

Scientists don't know how long a great white shark pregnancy lasts, but it's at least a year and a half. They think that females give birth every two to three years.

No one knows where pregnant white sharks hang out, but it's probably in warm water, as warmth helps the developing embryos grow faster.

BABY SHARKS

Great white sharks give birth to a small number of pups, which can be up to 1.5 metres long and weigh about 30 kilograms. The number of babies in a litter is usually between four and ten. They may have different fathers.

Great white sharks begin life as fertilised eggs, and they have their own yolk sac, which feeds them to start with. Then, as they grow, they begin to eat unfertilised eggs that their mother produces by the hundreds from her large ovaries. This is very different to human babies – and some other kinds of sharks – which are fed via a placenta while they're in their mother's womb.

White shark embryos have special sharp pointed baby teeth that they use to grab the egg capsules and then puncture them to suck out the yolk. Once they begin to eat the unfertilised eggs the young embryos grow quickly – but what grows the most is their stomach. They eat and eat, and the result is a hugely distended stomach that is so full of egg yolk it can be three-quarters of their body weight. It is so big that the muscles all along the shark's underside pull apart so the fat belly can poke out.

About halfway through the pregnancy, the mother stops producing eggs. As the baby sharks slowly use up all the yolk in their stomach, they store lots of that energy in their liver. This big, fatty liver will be what they live on for the first days after they are born until they learn to hunt.

The embryos lose their first sharp baby teeth and begin to produce new rows of teeth that are a different shape. These new teeth aren't useful yet as they are still folded flat. They won't stand up like real shark teeth until it is nearly time to be born. Embryonic sharks swallow most of the teeth that fall out as well as scales that they lose from their skin.

Their fat stomach slowly shrinks and the muscles knit back together, leaving a tiny scar on the baby shark's chest, which slowly fades. And what do they do with all the waste they produce from digesting all the eggs? They don't poo in the womb, so they store it up in their intestine ready for one almighty poo after they are born.

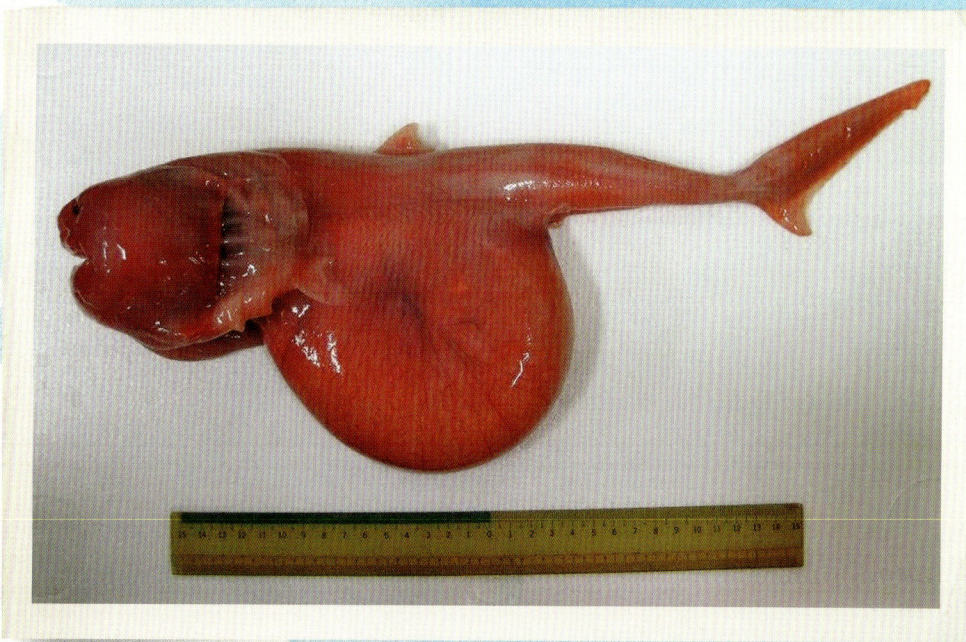

This embryo was one of more than 10 found in a pregnant 5-metre white shark killed in a fishing net off the coast of Taiwan. It was just over 40 centimetres long and weighed nearly 1.3 kilograms.

Chapter 10
PIP RETURNS

In June 2015, Malcolm is back at Stewart Island doing some winter shark fieldwork. He has chosen a different time of year from usual to see if bigger sharks turn up. But all he sees is the usual gang of mostly teenage boys.

He doesn't see Pip, but while he's there she sticks her fin, with its SPOT tag, above the water. It's a sure sign a shark is about to start travelling.

Sure enough, Pip heads south to the subantarctic again, but this time she goes to the Auckland Islands.

Malcolm wonders if she might be snacking on tasty New Zealand sea lion pups, which are becoming independent and learning to hunt for themselves.

But there are other possibilities, too. Midwinter is the time southern right whales gather at the northern end of the Auckland Islands to give birth and to mate. About 200 whales turn up every year. Whale calves, placenta and dead whales are all possible menu items for a hungry shark.

But Pip seems to be spending most of her time in deep water, and it seems more likely that she is eating fish, squid and maybe even deep-sea octopuses.

Her tag is sending only occasional pings and it's an agonising seven-week wait before another location beams in.

From: Malcolm Francis, NIWA
To: Clinton Duffy, Kina Scollay
Sent: 18 August 2015
Subject: Pip

Finally got a position from Pip. She's about 1/3 of the way between the Auckland Islands and Tasmania, so is well on her migration. Latitude about level with Stewart Island. Let's hope she continues to talk to us.

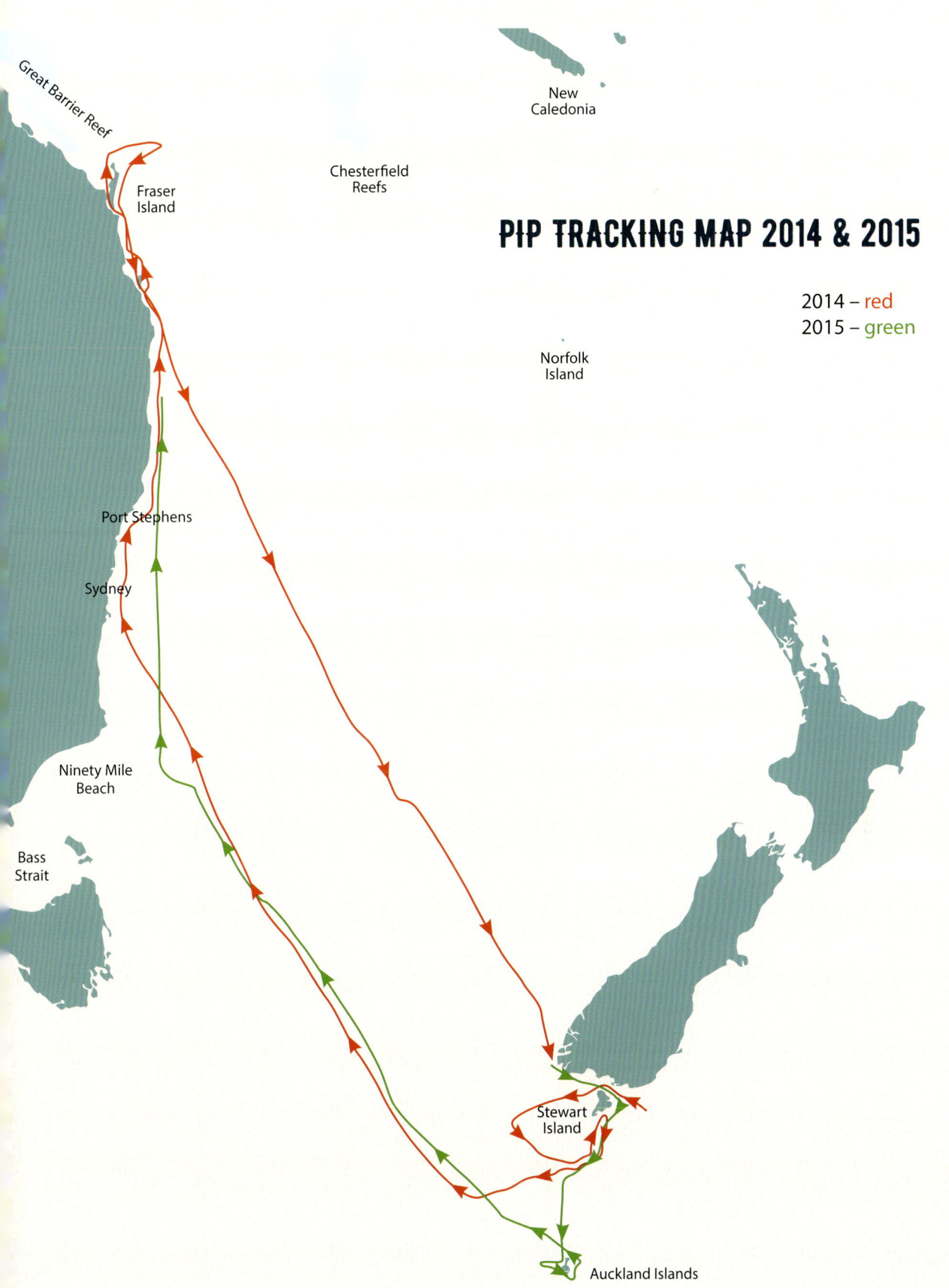

A week later she's back on almost exactly the same track she was following last year, which is one of those incredible shark talents. But the tag talk is unreliable and Malcolm worries that the tag is running out of battery.

In early September Pip reports in from northern New South Wales, then her tag falls silent. Clinton and Malcolm wonder if she's swimming up the coast again, aiming once more for the southern end of the Great Barrier Reef.

Pip was the last Stewart Island shark tagged and tracked during the New Zealand great white shark project. For now, she's still a teenager, with many years and many shark adventures ahead of her. The scientists had the privilege of having a snapshot of just 18 months of her life, but the rest of her life is a mystery. Where was she born? When she is old enough to have babies, will she go back there to give birth? How long will she live for, and where else might she travel to?

Over the 11 years of the New Zealand great white shark project, the scientists have added some important pieces to the great white shark puzzle – but there are many missing pieces, and lots more exciting discoveries still to be made by the shark scientists of the future.

Michael the great white shark was named in memory of Michael Manning. He was tagged with a PAT tag at Stewart Island in March 2011, when he was about 3.3 metres long. After three months the tag began to send a signal back to base, and Malcolm was intrigued because he could see on Google Earth that the signal was coming from a house in the country near Invercargill, and not from the sea.

Through a bit of detective work on the internet, Malcolm tracked down a phone number for the house. It belonged to a commercial fisher who had found the tag caught up in one of his fishing nets in Foveaux Strait. Naughty Michael the great white shark was probably trying to steal fish from the net! Malcolm was disappointed that he didn't find out where Michael had swum to, but he was relieved to hear that the shark had survived his encounter with the fishing net. And the fisher, in turn, was pleased he hadn't ended up with a white shark accidentally caught in his net, and he was glad to be able to return the shark tag to the scientists.

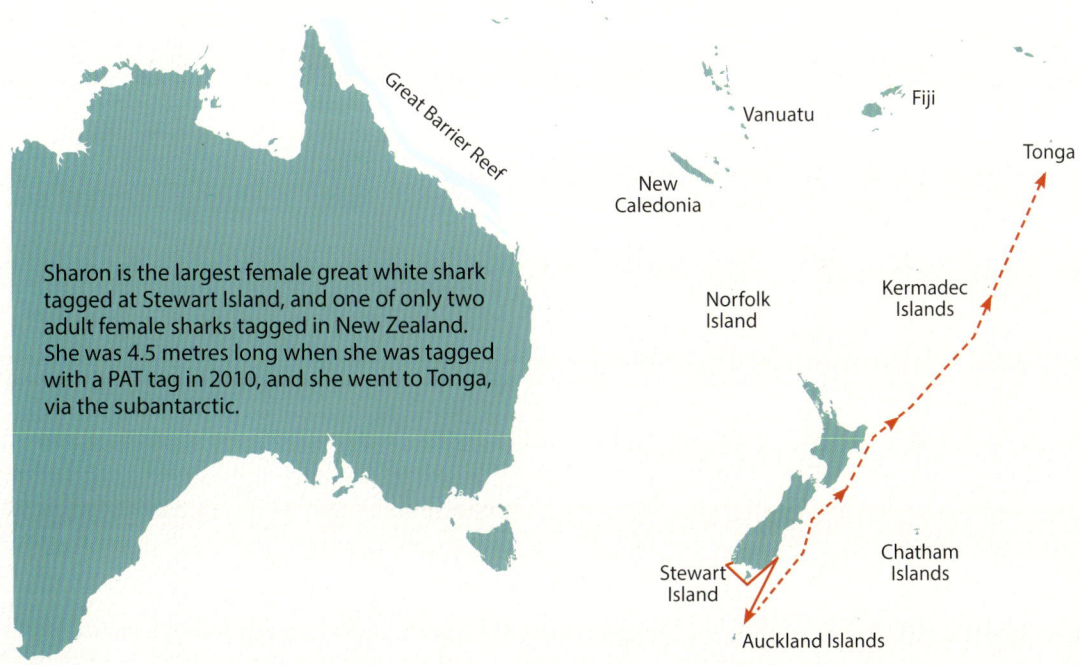

Sharon is the largest female great white shark tagged at Stewart Island, and one of only two adult female sharks tagged in New Zealand. She was 4.5 metres long when she was tagged with a PAT tag in 2010, and she went to Tonga, via the subantarctic.

The Numbers Game

How many great white sharks are there? Just like everything to do with great white sharks, it's very hard to answer.

One way is to count sharks at one place over a few days, take note of how many you recognise and how many are strangers. You also record how many times the sharks you know turn up. If you did this at school for a few days you'd be able to come up with a good estimate of how big the school roll is.

The tricky bit is that when more than half of the sharks haven't been seen before, and many sharks are only seen for one or two years, this makes it more like trying to count people at a busy railway station than a school.

By 2016, Clinton had identified more than 170 sharks at Stewart Island, and each year that number increases. He says that the most sharks he's ever identified at Stewart Island in one year was 59 animals, in 2015. He is still working out how big the Stewart Island population is.

And what about all of New Zealand? We know that the Stewart Island shark gang has lots of teenage boys and young adult males. What about the rest? We need to add in all the babies and juvenile sharks and the big adult sharks, and we don't know where these are or how many of them there are.

To make it even more complicated we also have to remember that east Australia and New Zealand's great white sharks are probably related and mix together.

What is clear is that, worldwide, the number of great white sharks is not big, and it is probably much smaller than it used to be.

When you don't have many sharks left, killing even a few of them is a big problem. White sharks die every year in beach protection nets in Australia and South Africa, and they are accidentally killed by recreational fishers and commercial fishing boats around the world. Great white sharks are protected in a few countries, but we now know that they spend lots of time swimming in international waters where they aren't well protected.

A healthy ocean needs a healthy population of sharks, and we've still got lots of work ahead of us to better understand and better protect these magnificent predatory fish.

Chapter 11
PIECES OF THE PUZZLE

WHAT WE KNOW

New Zealand great white sharks are nomads that roam around the southwest Pacific.

They spend about four months of the year in New Zealand, from late summer to early winter.

When they are in New Zealand, teenage sharks and some adult males spend lots of time at shark hotspots near New Zealand fur seal colonies, at Stewart Island and the Chatham Islands.

In spring, from September to December, there are hardly any sharks at Stewart Island.

Once they are big enough, New Zealand white sharks make long oceanic round trips of up to 9500 kilometres. These trips take about a month each way.

They often swim in a straight line and may follow the exact same route year after year (but not always).

They swim at about 4–5 kilometres per hour.

They spend six months of each year in subtropical and tropical waters, and seem to return to the same place each year.

Some sharks also go down to the subantarctic and spend weeks in cold water at places such as the Auckland Islands.

During their ocean trips great whites make frequent deep dives. They can reach depths of more than 1200 metres. They spend lots of time right at the surface.

White sharks can tolerate temperatures as cold as 2.7°C and as hot as 26.6°C.

New Zealand white sharks and east Australian white sharks are probably one big 'family'. Many tagged New Zealand sharks go to Australia, and tagged Australian sharks come to New Zealand.

In Australia, scientists think they know where great whites are born, and they have found two nursery areas.

Stewart Island and Chatham Island white sharks overlap and probably meet in the Pacific and eastern Australia, but there are no records of them moving between the two island groups in New Zealand.

UNSOLVED PUZZLE PIECES

We know *where* New Zealand's great white sharks go, but we don't know *why*.

We have no idea how great white sharks find their way across thousands of kilometres of ocean and back again.

We don't know what they do in the tropics.

We don't know where all the adult females and most of the adult males spend most of their time.

We don't know where adults meet up and mate, or what happens during shark sex.

We haven't found any pupping grounds or nursery areas around New Zealand, and there may be more nurseries to discover in Australia.

We don't know why white sharks dive to great depths – is it to feed on deep-ocean squid and fish?

We don't know how many great white sharks live around New Zealand.

ACKNOWLEDGEMENTS

I had the amazing opportunity, in 2012, to spend a couple of days out on the water at Stewart Island with the New Zealand great white shark research team. I had always thought that great white sharks were rather over-rated and over-hyped (they're just a shark, after all, and I've had the privilege of diving with a number of different shark species). But when the first great white appeared alongside the boat I was awe-struck. She was so big, so graceful and, as she swam past at the surface, staring up at us with dark, expressionless eyes, sizing us up, I felt very firmly put in my place.

I have been equally struck by great white shark science, and it's been a privilege to watch it unfold over the last few years.

This book wouldn't have been possible without the support of Malcolm Francis, from NIWA, and Clinton Duffy, from the Department of Conservation, who allowed me to tell the story of their research, and who patiently shared data and anecdotes. Huge thanks, too, to all the members of the New Zealand great white shark project team, for their work over the years: Kina Scollay, Warrick Lyon, Steve 'Meadsy' Meads, Clint 'Barney' Brown, Phred Dobbins, the late Michael Manning, Tim Gregory-Hunt, Ramon Bonfil, Sharon Pasco, Pip Green and many others. Many of the sharks that feature in the book were named after them and their families.

A big thank you, also, to Barry Bruce, from CSIRO in Australia, for sharing his knowledge and experience.

I have written this book as a story but it is totally based on science and fact. The emails in the book, for example, are genuine emails, and I have pedantically trawled through tagging data to make sure I have got everything correct. That said, if there are any errors they are entirely my fault and nobody else's.

A big shout-out to the photographers, especially Mark Enarson, whose photos make this book look so incredible. All of the photos in the book are of New Zealand sharks, and they really are who we say they are.

I take my hat off to the wonderful team at Potton & Burton for sharing my vision, and making the book look more magnificent than I could have imagined. Thanks to Robbie Burton, Louise Belcher, Alan Bridgland and Karen Jones, and to Chris Chisnall for his design concept, as well as Jude Watson.

Thanks to the generosity of the Michael Manning Memorial Trust, hundreds of copies of this book have been given to school libraries in New Zealand and the South Pacific. Caitlin, Juliette, John, and Judy and Eddie – this is for you, in memory of Michael.

To my partner, Malcolm Francis, thank you for your love, patience and encouragement.

Writing this book made me realise that the real world is more fascinating than anything we can dream up, and I hope it inspires you all to stand up for sharks and look after our fascinating marine environment.

GLOSSARY

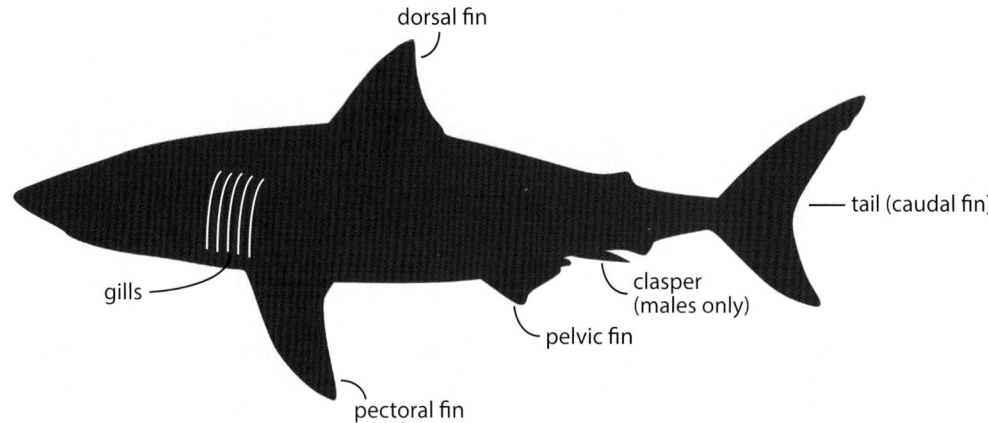

clasper – male sharks have two claspers – long sausage-shaped sex organs – that sit along the inside edge of the pelvic fins. The claspers are used to deposit sperm into the cloaca of female sharks.

cloaca – both male and female sharks have a cloaca, located on their belly between their pelvic fins. It is the opening for excreting urine and faeces and, in males, for sperm to come out of. In female sharks it is the equivalent of a vagina.

dorsal fin – the large fin on the shark's back that is often seen when a shark comes to the water's surface. The dorsal fin keeps a shark stable while it is swimming. SPOT tags are attached to the dorsal fin.

electroreceptor – specialised sensory organs located on a shark's snout. This network of jelly-filled pores, called ampullae of Lorenzini, detects electrical signals given off by other animals. The electroreceptors help sharks locate prey, and it is possible that they may also help them navigate. Salt water is very good at conducting electricity.

gills – slits located behind a shark's head and in front of the pectoral fins that they use to 'breathe'. Sharks take in water through their mouth and extract oxygen from it as the water flows across their gills.

pectoral fin – the large fins on each side of the shark that keep it afloat and also help it to turn and to angle up or down.

pelvic fin – the pair of small fins located near the shark's tail, which help with stability.

predator – an animal that preys on other animals. Great white sharks are the largest predatory fish in the world.

tail – also known as the caudal fin, the tail sweeps from side to side to propel the shark through the water.

INDEX

Page numbers in **bold** refer to photos and maps.

acoustic listening stations **17**, 34–35, 38
acoustic tags 16, **16**, 17, 20, **20**, 23, 34–35, **35**, 38
age of great white sharks 32–33
Alison (shark) **24–25**, 25
Atlantic Ocean 56, 57, **57**, 67
attacks by great white sharks 13, 14, 23, 46, 61
Auckland Islands 29, 38, 72, **73**, **75**, 78
Australia 28, 56, **56**, 57, **59**, 61, 63–64, 67, **73**, 77, 78, 79
    great white shark project 64–65
    shark nurseries 65–66, 78

baby great white sharks 70–71
    see also young great white sharks
berley 18, 19, **19**, 42
body temperature 25, 51
Bondi Line 38
Bonfil, Ramon 14
breeding grounds 66, 69, 78, 79
Bruce (shark) 38
Bruce, Barry 64, **64**, 65, 66

cages **36**, 36–37, 60
Campbell Island 29
Caro (shark) 17, **26–27**, 27
Chatham Islands 13, 14, 15, **15**, 16, 31, 78, 79
Chesterfield Reefs, Coral Sea **15**, 28, 29, 38, 45, 51, **59**
Cook Islands 51
counting great white sharks 77
CSIRO (Commonwealth Scientific and Industrial Research Organisation) 64

Darby, John 40
Dave (shark) 31, **52–53**, 53
deep diving 16, 29, 30, 35, 48–49, 50, 53, 55, 66, 78, 79
Department of Conservation 11, 18, 31, 45, 60
dermal denticles 25, **25**
diet of great white sharks 18–19, 40, **40**, **41**, 51, 72, 79
distribution of great white sharks **56–57**
DNA research 67
    see also genetics

Dobbins, Phred 45
Duffy, Clinton 9, 11, **11**, **14**, **34**

Edwards Island 18–19, 35, 36, 45, 51
eggs 71
electronic tags 9, 10, 14, 15, **16**, 16–17, 21, **22**, 23, 28–29, 42–45, **44**, 62, **63**, 64
    see also acoustic tags; PAT tags; SPOT tags
electroreceptors 24
Ella (shark) 21, 23, 28–29, **29**, 35
embryos 69, 70, 71, **71**
Emer (shark) 38
eyesight 24, 46, 55

fish, in the diet of great white sharks 40, 51, 55, 72, 75, 79
food eaten by great white sharks 18–19, 40, **40**, **41**, 51, 72, 79
Foveaux Strait 34–35, 45
Francis, Malcolm 9, 12, **12**, **19**, **22**
Fraser Island, Australia 38, **59**, **73**
Fraser, Mike 29

genetics 42, 47, 67
    see also DNA
gills 26, 42, 44, 49, 68
Great Barrier Reef, Australia 28, 61, 66, 74
Gregory-Hunt, Tim 14, 31
Grim (shark) 17
growth rings in vertebra 69–70

Hawks Nest, Australia 64, 65
hunting by great white sharks 46, **46**, **47**, 55

identifying sharks 26
Indian Ocean 56, **56**
International Shark Attack File (ISAF) 61

Jane (shark) 33
journeys made by great white sharks 14, **15**, 28, 29, 50, 51, 56, **56–57**, 57, 66, 67, 78, 79
    Ella's journey 28–29, **29**
    Nicholas Cage's journeys 9, 48–49, 50, 58, **59**, 60
    Pip's journeys 63–64, 68, 72, **73**, 74, **74**
    Sharon's journey 75, **75**

Kaipara Harbour 66
Kara (shark) 28
Kermadec Islands 14, 51, **51**
Kerri (shark) 29, **30**

lateral line 25
Lifou Island 49
Livie (shark) 17
locations of great white sharks 56, **56–57**, 57
Lyon, Warrick 17

Manning, Michael **14**, 75
Manukau Harbour 66
map of great white shark locations **56–57**
Marbletail (shark, nickname 'Bling Boy') 31, **35**, 38, **38**
Meadsy (shark) 38
Meadsy (skipper) 18, 23
Meca (shark) 14, **15**, 31
Mediterranean Sea 56, **56**, 67
Michael (shark) 75, **75**
Miller, Roger 31

National Institute of Water and Atmospheric Research (NIWA) 12
navigation by great white sharks 50
New Caledonia 14, **15**, 31, 48, 51, 53
Nicholas Cage (shark, Nic for short) 9, **9**, 17, 23, 35, 36–37, **43**, 43–45, **44**
  disappearance 60
  journey back to New Zealand from Pacific 58, **59**, 60
  journey to the Pacific 9, 48–49, 50, **59**
Nicole (shark) 14, 56
Ninety Mile Beach, Australia **59**, 65, 66
Niue 51
North America 56, 57, **57**
number of great white sharks 77, 79

octopuses 72

Pacific Ocean and islands 10, 14, **15**, 28, 56, 57, **57**, **59**, 67, 75, **75**, 78, 79
PAT tags (Pop-up Archival Transmitting tags) 14, 16, **16**, 20, 23, 28–29, 38, 45, **61**, 75
  lost tags 14, 16, **16**, 20, 23, 28–29
Phred (shark) **36–37**, 45, **45**
Pip (shark) 17, 62–64, **63**, 66, 68, 72, **73**, 74, **74**
populations of great white sharks 56, **56–57**, 57, 77, 79
Port Stephens, Australia **59**, 65–66, **73**
pregnancy 69–70, **70**
protection of great white sharks 60, 77

satellite monitoring 9, 16, 17, 60
Scollay, Kina 9, 13, **13**
sea lions (New Zealand) 29, **30**, 72

seals (New Zealand fur) 18–19, 40, **41**, 46, 60
sensory pores 25
sex 38, 68–69, 79
Shack (shark) 33, 61, **61**
Shared Foraging Offshore Area (SOFA) 57
Shark Café 57
shark cages **36**, 36–37, 60
Sharon (shark) 33, 75, **75**
sizes of great white sharks **32–33**, 61, 75
  compared to a man 33
skin 25, **25**
smell, great white shark's sense 24, 46, 50, 55
Sound Fixing and Ranging (SOFAR) channel 55
South Africa 56, **56**, 67, 77
SPOT tags (Smart Position or Temperature Transmitting tags) 9, 17, **17**, 27, **27**, 42–45, **44**, 48, 62, **63**, 72
squid 40, 41, 55, 57, 72, 79
Star Keys/Motuhope 14
Stewart Island 14, 16, 17, 34, 35, 42, 51, 58, **59**, 60, 61, 62, 64, **73**, **75**, 77, 78, 79
  shark gang 38, 77
subantarctic islands 29, 30, 38, 72, 78
Swain's Reef, Australia 30
swimming, great white sharks 25, 78

tagging sharks 9, 10, 14, 15, 16–17, 21, **22**, 23, 28–29, 42–45, **44**, 62, **63**, 64
Tasman Sea **59**, 63–64, **73**
taste buds 46
teeth 39, **39**, 40, 46, **47**
temperature of stomachs and muscles 25
Tessa (shark) 14, **15**
Tim (shark) 31
Titi Islands 18–19, 35
Tonga 31, 51, **75**
Tristan (shark) 14, **15**
tropics 14, 15, 51, 64, 66, 78, 79
tuna 20, 51

Vanuatu 14, **15**

Western Australia 14, 56, **56**, 65
whale blubber 40
whales 51, **51**, 55, 72

young great white sharks
  see also baby great white sharks
  Australia 65–66
  New Zealand 66, 67

83

PHOTO CREDITS

Dave Abbott: page 30 (bottom); Dave Allen/NIWA: page 19; Ross Armstrong: pages 24–25; Patricia Danna/Biosphoto: page 41 (bottom); Steve Dawson: back endpaper; Clinton Duffy: pages 16 (bottom), 35, 44 (left); CSIRO: page 64; Mark Enarson: cover, pages 4–5, 10–11, 21, 26–27, 36–37, 38, 39, 40–41, 45, 46, 47, 50, 54–55, 67, 69, 74, 76–77, 79; Malcolm Francis: pages 2, 11, 14, 15, 16 (top), 17 (top), 17 (bottom), 40, 44 (right), 52–53; Steve Hathaway: page 51; Dave Harasti: page 65; Hua Hsun Hsu: page 71; Warrick Lyon: pages 12, 20, 22, 34, 63; Lee & Roger Miller: page 31; Jenny (Maria) Oliver: page 13; Steve O'Shea: page 41 (top); Kina Scollay: pages 29, 43, 61, 75; Daniel Scott: page 70; Peter Scott: page 9; Rob Suisted (Naturespic): page 30 (top); University of Cape Town: page 25.

The publisher gratefully acknowledges the support of the Michael Manning Memorial Trust in the production of this book.

First published in 2017 by Potton & Burton
98 Vickerman Street, PO Box 5128, Nelson, New Zealand
pottonandburton.co.nz

Text © Alison Ballance
Photography © Individual photographers

ISBN 978 0 47503 18 5

Printed in China by Midas Printing International Ltd

This book is copyright. Apart from any fair dealing for the purposes of private study, research, criticism or review, as permitted under the Copyright Act, no part may be reproduced by any process without the permission of the publisher.